The Strawplaiters of Orkney

Fiona Grahame

Dedicated to my sister Catriona McBean

The Orkney News

First published in Scotland by Orkney News Ltd., Orkney, 2023.

The Orkney News is free to read online at theorkneynews.scot

© Orkney News Ltd. 2023.

Cover illustration © Martin Laird, 2023. Used with permission.

ISBN 978-1-9196105-2-8

Contents

Introduction

"On her head she wore a great straw bonnet, with trimmings of the same, in which she looked as if she had been thatched by an unskilful labourer." [1]

People have been plaiting straw since the earliest of times and using it to make all sorts of useful items like baskets, mats and head wear. A Palaeolithic-Mesolithic cave site in Coves de Santa Maira, Spain, has produced evidence of braided plant fibres and basketry imprints on clay. [2]

In the 19th century the production of straw hats was caught up in the industrial fervour of the time and saw a cottage industry develop into a mass employer of women with a complex supply and distribution chain. The English town of Luton, near London, was to eventually become the centre for the straw hat trade. Unlikely as it may seem, Orkney, in the northern isles of Scotland, was also well known for strawplait and bonnet making during the first half of the 19th century. There were many similarities between the development of the industry in Orkney and in other centres of its production, but also major differences.

In the research for this account I have used the published census for 1821, 1841 and 1851; The Statistical Accounts of Orkney; newspaper reports; letters and archival records. Recorded ages of individuals and the spelling of their names can vary. I am indebted to the superb local resources and the staff of Orkney Library and Archive and The Orkney Family and History Society, in being able to piece together some of the lives described in this account.

I apologise for any mistakes which may have been made in my research for the lives of women for whom there is very little written record.

This account describes the strawplaiting industry in Britain in the 19th century and sets within that what happened in Orkney for the first half of that century.

Fiona Grahame

Straw Plaiting in England

From the mid 1600s people were plaiting straw and making straw hats in rural parts of England, for example, Bedfordshire and Buckinghamshire.

"By the late 1600s straw plaiting and hat making had become an important part of the local economy. In 1689 the straw plaiters of Bedfordshire, Hertfordshire and Buckinghamshire were confident enough in their industry and its importance to petition Parliament. The petition of 1719 … protests against imported plaits and hats. This was to become a problem for many generations of plaiters and hatters." [3]

Fine Italian plait provided the material for expensive straw hats from the 1700s onwards. English straw was much coarser and it was used for the cheaper end of the market. War with Napoleonic France interrupted supplies of imports. In England, this led to better methods of producing the plait. Splitting of the homegrown coarser material meant it could be plaited into something similar to the Italian plait. Even after the ending of the war in 1815, duties on imports continued to be of advantage to the home producers. Straw plaiting and with it the straw bonnet industry flourished in many parts of rural England with trading taking place at straw markets in the main towns.

It was a rural industry dominated by low paid work for women and children. There were even 'plait schools' set up in these regions with children as young as 3 working in crowded and cramped cottages. Parents paid a fee for the child to attend and a mistress kept them at their work. Parents would then be paid by how much plait their child had produced. The women who ran the plait schools were supposed to teach basic reading and writing but the plaiting of straw took priority. Most often very little 'education' took place.

"Inside the schools the children were seated on stools or forms, and during the winter months there were often so many of them in the room that they encroached upon the fireplace and made it impossible for a fire to be lit." [4]

There were different designs of plaited straw, the successful execution of which was dependent upon the quality of the straw and the skill of the plaiter.

"A ten year old child was expected to make about 30 yards a day if the plait was a simple one. Intricate plaits could fetch high prices but took longer to make. Plait was usually sold by the score which was 20 yards. An average week's earnings from plaiting was five shillings." [5]

The plaiting of straw could take place in the home, but also in small workshops where workers were crowded together. Traders would travel to the towns and villages buying up the plait to take to one of the bigger market places. In 1860, Luton's straw plait market was so busy that in January 1869 the purpose-built Plait Halls were opened to bring the market indoors.

"In 1842 tariffs on imported straw were reduced, causing trade depression, but the damage was not permanent. In the longer term, the English industry successfully weathered the storm of foreign competition through to the 1870s, producing a bewildering variety of new plaits that competed effectively with Italian imports despite the abolition of protective duties".[6]

Although, "imports of plait increased from an average of 25,244 lbs. per annum in 1830-35 to 138,267 lbs. in the period 1865-70" [7], there was an increase in exports to the USA.

In Orkney by the late 1850s the industry had flourished and then as quickly it had vanished.

Straw Plaiting in Orkney

Located on the ground floor of the Stromness Museum is an unassuming rare object. It is a piece of strawplait made by Mrs J Rendall . Sitting next to it in the glass case is the medal she won at the 1851 Great Exhibition in London.

It is a beautiful piece of skilled straw work and one of the few remaining pieces of evidence left of an industry which over a span of half a century employed thousands of women in Orkney.

The industry was very successful but why did it come about in the first place ? What led it to be established in Orkney and, when it collapsed, what happened to all those it had employed ?

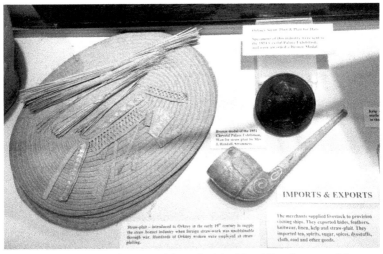

Straw plait & medal won by Mrs J Rendall in Stromness Museum.

Orkney's Straw

Straw was once the choice material for Orcadians which they skilfully twisted and prepared for a myriad of uses around the farmstead. Gone now are most of those skills as are most of the Orcadian words that went with the production of straw goods.

Straw is a by-product of cereal plants: barley, oats, rye, wheat and rice. Black oats was one of the most common varieties grown in Orkney and its fine flexible stalks were excellent for making straw goods.

Straw products were an essential part of the Orkney farmstead. Everything from the furniture you sat on, to the roof over your head and the basket the peats were in for the fire, was made from straw.

The Orkney chair is today recognised as a quality piece of furniture with a price that reflects the skill that has gone into making it. Originally it was made entirely out of straw until a North Ronaldsay man took some wood that had washed ashore and adapted the design to have a wooden seat. Over time changes were made with wooden arms and a drawer – the guidman's stuil – where the heid o' the hoose would keep his tobacco and copies of books.

Its construction from straw and driftwood meant it was considered to be for the poorer type of house. The back of the chair is made from flexible oat straw, built up in regular courses less than an inch thick. All the courses (45 of them) were originally bound together with bent grass but today it is thin straw-coloured cord.

The importance of having a successful farm and bringing in a good harvest had many traditions involving straw. In the parish of Sandwick when a man was to start his own farm he received a gift of sheaves from his neighbours. This was called 'sheaf getting'.

Bringing in the last of the harvest was especially important. A 'bikko' (from the Old Norse bikkja) was a straw dog. It was made from the last of the straw gathered and hoisted onto a prominent position in the stackyard – usually at the top of the farm building. Over time this tradition changed to become a form of insult. The bikko was put up on the house of the man who was the last to get his harvest in.

Another tradition involved two short straws being placed in the fire. They are given the names of a lad and a lass and placed on a glowing peat. On one straw is a knot. Soon the heat will cause the straw to jump slightly. If it jumps towards the other straw then this is seen as an omen that the named lad and lass will be wed.

There are many different Orcadian words for the huge variety of straw products which were made:

The 'bent' (straw) was bound into neat 'baets' which were 2 spans in circumference. Each baet was carefully plaited together gradually tapering to end in a cord which allowed two baets to be tied together.

2 baets = band of bent

12 bands of bent = a thraive

From the baets could be made cords of varying thicknesses – the thickest being tether bands to the finest stuile bands.

Simmans: these were straw ropes which involved a double twist making them strong. The double twist also acted against each other, preventing unravelling. It was wound into a clew.

Clew: wound in such a way that the end in the middle of the ball was accessible. It was as big as could fit through the barn door where it was kept until it was needed.

Simmans were used to thatch the roof and were laid in close parallel lines from eave to eave.

Sookans: a simple straw rope of a single twist. These were used for tying down stacks – perhaps 30 ropes for one stack.

Strae-buits: straw rope was wound under the instep of the boot, over the top and round the leg to the knee. An excellent way for the wearer to keep warm in winter. 'Such straw boots formed the most comfortable part of a peasant's dress.' – Walter T Dennison

The whole of the farm horse's harness was formed from straw. Sitherhips (britchen): were formed by plaiting bent cord into a thin, broad belt.

Maze: this was made by working the cord into a net. Sheaves would then be suspended on each side of the horse in the maze at harvest time.

Wazzie: the horse collar – this was formed by twisting 4 thick folds of straw together.

For the house, there were straw products galore of every conceivable size.

Flackies were mats where the straw was bound together with bent cord. Small ones might be on the floor by the side of the bed, larger ones could be hung over doorways to keep out drafts.

Flackies were used at kiln doors during the grain drying process. They were also used on horses to protect the animal's back when carrying heavy loads.

The bed mattress – palliasse – was also most likely filled with straw.

Beek: this was a large number of flackies sewn together to make a long web of straw matting. It was rolled out and with its sides stitched together formed a large circular 'vessel'. This was used to store grain and all held together by simmans neatly rolled around its outer side. The final beek would be thatched all over and form a cone shape.

Miels kaesie: these were of a closer texture than the flackies and made into a large bag or sometimes as a flexible oval shaped basket. After being filled it would be laced closed.

Miels kaesies filled with grain were used to pay the rent. They were also used to carry the grain to the mill and return with the meal, all transported by horse. The horses were tied to the tail of the horse in front. One man would attend every 2 horses or so always checking that the kaesies remained balanced each side of the animal. There could be 20 or 30 horses involved on some journeys.

Corn kaesie: this was barrel shaped and stood in the barn where it was used for holding dressed grain. It came in a variety of sizes.

Common kaesie: this was for carrying burdens on your back. It was narrow and rounded at the bottom. At the top was a fesgar, a circular rim. To the fesgar were fastened two ends of a bent rope. This was called the fettle. The kaesie was suspended from the shoulders of the bearer whilst his arm was placed through the hoop. If it was a long journey the fettle would be placed over both shoulders. Young children were often carried in kaesies by their mothers.

Cubbies: these were slightly smaller than kaesies but were firm, and varied in shape.

Window cubbie: this is a cubbie from which corn is dropped while being winnowed.

There were also the following: Kiln cubbie; Sawin cubbie; Hen cubbie; Ass cubbie; Sea cubbie: for carrying fish; Bait cubbie: for carrying bait; Horse cubbie: a muzzle used on the horse; and Spoon cubbie: hung at the side of the fireplace.

Beggars carried cubbies too and to say a man would have "to take to the cubbie and the staff" was to infer that he would become a beggar.

Luppie: a basket for dry goods, eggs and meal. It could be from 10 inches in height to 3 ft. A luppie had a rim round the lower end to protect the bottom and two lugs on opposite sides at the top. The smallest ones would be used as work baskets by the guid wife. Luppies and straw stools tended to have the finest straw work done on them. [8]

There was, therefore, a traditional skill set of working with straw already established which the manufacturers and traders in straw plait could utilise immediately.

When the industry started in the islands, at the beginning of the 19th century, the whole process could take place in Orkney: from the harvesting of the straw, plaiting it into lengths, sewing these together into a bonnet and finally shipping them south to the big ports like Liverpool.

Over the course of its 50+ years of manufacture this sector employed thousands of women, some in 'workshops', and others in their own homes.

There were islands in Orkney where there was either none, or very little, involvement in the industry: for instance North Ronaldsay where there are no records of strawplaiting taking place. This is not surprising considering the difficulties of transport from that island and other means of employing the tenanted farmers.

The Orkney straw from black oats was excellent for the production of fine quality flexible material. Soon demand from the industry exceeded what the islands could produce and there were years when the harvest was poor, so straw had to be imported.

The statistical accounts for 1842 record that in Sandwick those employed at plaiting the straw could earn 6d a day. Although the majority of this work was done by young, single women, the age range spanned across the generations: from age 5 to 75. Many of these women worked all their lives in female only households, with men either at sea, working away from home, in the services, or who had died leaving widows with very little income. For those women on such low finances, marriage prospects were poor and they were to remain unmarried.

As the century entered its second half, Orkney struggled to compete with cheaper products made nearer the mass markets. Wages were lowered and when the industry collapsed the income which hundreds of poorer women had relied upon in Orkney went with it. When there was no longer an income to be made from plaiting, they got by earning money from knitting – mostly stockings. Women like Kirkwall's Jane Ferrier who was still earning from working in knitting when in her 70s.

There is very little evidence today of the highly skilled work these women did.

From those who plaited the straw the work was passed onto the bonnet makers. The bonnet makers tended to be young and single although many of them were later married. They often married into similar skilled trades such as shoemakers and tailors. When the industry collapsed many of these women became seamstresses and dressmakers. Jane Wallace, of Kirkwall, remained single and living with her sisters. They earned their income as dressmakers and milliners. Straw bonnet manufacturing may have vanished in Orkney but the skills of the seamstress and hat maker were still needed.

At the top of the pyramid of production were the manufacturers: the agents who imported the straw and exported the finished product. These were almost exclusively male and resided in the main towns of Kirkwall and Stromness. Men like William Heddle (Stromness) and George McBeath (Kirkwall) made great profits when the industry was at its height. If they were shrewd they moved those profits into other lines of business before the boom went bust.

In 1833 the annual income being generated in Orkney from its various interests and recorded by Rev Charles Clouston, Minister of Sandwick, was as follows:

- Herring: £170,000
- Whaling : £7,500
- Cod: £7,280
- Straw manufacture: £4,800
- Horses, Cows, Oxen: £4,290 (+ £1,104)
- Bere: £3,883
- Butter: £2,700
- Eggs: £2,500
- Kelp: £2,250
- Malt: £1,604
- Lobsters: £1,800
- Hudson's Bay: £1,500 (wages)
- White Oats: £909
- Rabbit Skins: £600
- Feathers: £250
- Sheep, Swine: £80
- Peas: £35 2/-
- Oatmeal: £28

The straw manufacturing industry was important because it gave women paid employment, in cash.

It has been suggested that the demise of the industry in Orkney was due to Queen Victoria making fun of a gift she had been given of a straw hat. It is said that as a fashion setter that once the Queen mocked the straw hat, women stopped buying them. This is simply incorrect. Although the manufacture of straw plait disappears from Orkney in the second half of the 19th century, this is not the case in the rest of the UK. The industry may have died out in Orkney but

with Free Trade and a growing Empire it thrived in England.
In an account of the making of straw bonnets in New Zealand, the
author tells us that:

"The English plait trade was concentrated in Bedfordshire,
Buckinghamshire and Hertfordshire, counties that offered the best
growing conditions for wheat. Established as early as the seventeenth
century, this trade was in decline from the 1870s." [9]

Later on in the 19th century cheap imports of straw had come in
from China. Long strands which could be used on machines. The
industry had become mechanised. It became centralised in Luton
where the hats continued to be made in factories.

Straw plait display in Orkney Museum, Kirkwall.

Orkney has the Raw Materials

Britain was at war with Napoleonic France from 1803 to 1815. War interferes with trade and it did so in the case of supplying leghorn straw for the manufacture of straw bonnets. The solution was to grow your own.

Orkney's lairds and merchants had grown wealthy out of the two industries of kelp and linen.

"Between 1801 and 1806 the manufacture of linen cloth dropped by one third and the export of spindles of yarn was down by more than a half…In 1808 there was 'widespread distress' among the linen-makers in Holm…Some linen was still being made in Orkney in 1823 , but by 1830 it was stone dead." [10]

The kelp industry had also collapsed. Kelp (seaweed tangles) was gathered and fired in pits. The material left had the chemical composition to be used in the making of soap. It was an extremely lucrative industry: the kelp was on the shoreline and the tenants of the landowners had to collect and process it. When this was no longer profitable landowners and merchants had to seek another product to fill this gap. The strawplait and bonnet making industry was born.

Orkney had everything that was needed: the raw materials, the skilled, cheap workforce and the shipping agents who would transport the finished product to markets in the south. Orkney's crop of black oats produced a straw which had fine flexible stalks. Landowners such as William Watt at Skaill, also experimented with importing grains to improve the existing crop.

"The only crop cultivated for the arts is rye, for making bonnets, 9 acres of which are raised by Mr Watt, at what appears a liberal rent of £6.10s per acre, but he has to manure and work the land, and furnish carts whenever they are required, for carrying the produce to the boiler, thence to the bleaching field, and then to Kirkwall, or Stromness." [11]

Leghorn straw could be grown in Orkney in small quantities but was not anywhere near enough to supply the demand. It was a yellow colour and very much preferred for the making of straw bonnets. Importing leghorn straw had a boost when in 1842 the high duties from Italy were reduced to be eventually abolished in 1860. This meant the industry's requirements in Orkney could be met by importing the raw materials without the worry of the local harvest not providing enough.

"The raw material is either Tuscan straw imported….or rye straw raised in Orkney, which is more durable, and very little inferior in appearance." [12]

The harvesting and processing of the straw before it could be plaited took a considerable time. In The Dundee Advertiser 17th August 1898, William Bews a Kirkwall grocer, recalls how the straw was harvested for the Kirkwall manufacturer, David Ramsay.

"The straw was grown largely on the farms of Seatter, Cleat and Holland, on the east side of Kirkwall. When grown to its full height, and while still green , it was cut down in small hand bundles. It was then spread out on the hill of Seatter to bleach in the rain, wind and sun until it became white. It was afterwards carted into Kirkwall and stored, dressed and dyed in Mr Ramsay's stores. It was then bound into hand bundles of 50 to the sheaf and given to the workers to be plaited into hats, mats and other articles for domestic use. These were returned to the agent when completed. So great was the traffic in the giving out and receiving of these articles that Mr Bews had seen the road almost blocked with people waiting their turns… Ready money was given to all who wished it on the return of their work, but many who preferred their money to lie in Mr Ramsay's hands received a ticket with the amount due to them, to be drawn at their convenience." [13]

The straw could be made into finer strips by splitting. From around 1800 a machine was developed which could help split the straw. The machines were simple devices and relatively cheap to purchase at 6d each.

The process was not without its health implications, especially if sulphur had to be used to bleach it.

"Straw plaiting was also a risk to health. The process involved taking strands of specially prepared, bleached and flattened straw then plaiting it by hand into strips. The straws could be brittle and had to be dampened to stop them splitting, usually by swiping the straw through the mouth. The straw often had traces of sulphur on it, a residue of the bleaching process. Frequently fingers and mouths were cut. In the later half of the nineteenth century, evidence began to accumulate of the risk to health. The death rate amongst women who plaited straw was almost 50% higher than in the population of women as a whole. Straw plaiters were more likely to die of tuberculosis and cancers of the mouth and throat were more common. The Children's Employment Commission found children introduced to straw plaiting were more likely to be feeble and retarded in their development." [14]

The Straw Plaiters of Orkney

In The New History of Orkney, William P.L. Thomson, states that the straw plaiting industry was introduced into Orkney in 1804 by Mr Larking, a London bonnet maker and was then quickly taken up by traders who saw how it could turn into a profitable enterprise for them. [15]

In the parish of Birsay women were soon employed plaiting straw.

'The chief employment of the females, now, is straw plaiting; which was introduced into the parish, in the year 1807 by Mr Robert Borwick, Kirkwall.' [16]

The industry found in Orkney an abundant supply of cheap skilled female labour, merchants who knew a good thing when it came along and an efficient shipping sector for imports and exports. By 1833 it was worth £4,800 in income to Orkney – that's over half a million pounds today.

Women could earn 1 shilling 6 pence or 2 shillings weekly depended on how much plait they produced. According to Thomson, in The New History of Orkney, the women earned 3 to 6 pence a day.

The Rev. Thomas Blyth found that in the parishes of Birsay and Harray, "The quantity manufactured is considerable; but the annual value cannot be ascertained." [17]

The straw was plaited into lengths of braid, some would be sent south in bundles and some would be delivered to bonnet makers in Orkney. The Rev Logie noted:

"This kind of labour, as at present conducted by the agents giving out the straw to the women to be manufactured in their own dwellings, is not liable to the objection of injuring the morals, as in the case of manufactures which assemble multitudes of the young in one place." [18]

The 1841 census for Orkney records 1,282 women employed plaiting straw. The prevalence of the industry was different across the islands' parishes. There were high numbers of women employed in the towns of Kirkwall and Stromness. Women were also attracted into those towns by the chance of work as strawplaiters and bonnet makers. In some of the parishes too it had a high rate of employment, especially in Sandwick, Birsay and Harray.

By 1851 the number of women employed plaiting straw in Orkney had fallen to 673.

Those employed in the industry were nearly all women. They tended to be young and unmarried. To understand what was happening in Orkney, it is important to look at the individual parishes because the situation was different in each of them.

Birsay, West Mainland

"The number of landowners in the parish, resident and non-resident, is 39: of whom 10 are non-resident. The principal landowner is the Earl of Zetland, who is also patron of the parish." [19]

The Rev Blyth noted that improvements in farming were hampered by the short one year leases tenant farmers had in Birsay. The farms were mostly small, paying an annual rent of £8 or £9. Many of the men were employed in fishing, a dangerous job now and even more so then. As in other parishes of Orkney, young men sought employment as seafarers or with the Hudson Bay company in Canada.

"A considerable number of the young men go yearly to the Davis Straits, and also to Hudson's Bay."[20]

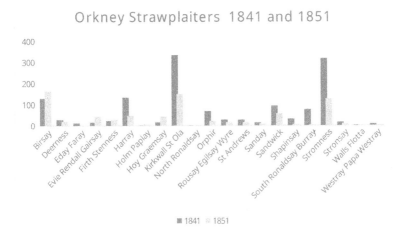

Orkney Strawplaiters 1841 and 1851

Women were left to run the farm and bring in such income as they could from industries such as straw plaiting.

In 1841, 128 women in Birsay were employed in straw plaiting, about 8% of a total population of 1,634. The youngest was 8 year old Ann Stickler and the oldest, 65 year old Mary Spence.

"It still forms the chief employment of the females, though their wages are much lower than they were, when it was first introduced." [21]

By this time children were attending one of the 6 schools listed in the parish and there was a library mainly of religious and moral books established in 1841.

"There are few or none under fifteen years of age in this parish, who cannot read or write." [22]

By the 1851 census Birsay's population had increased to 1,749 and 163 women were employed as strawplaiters: just over 9% of the total population and 17% of females in the parish. This is when the rest of Orkney was seeing a very marked decline in straw plaiting employment.

The youngest was Ann McDonald, 12 years old, and the oldest, a widow, 74 year old Elizabeth Marwick.

The 1851 census is also useful for giving us the marital status of the women.

- Single 143
- Married 13
- Widowed 8

Birsay had many poor people and itinerant workers residing in it during the first half of the 19th century. They were employed plaiting straw and living in very poor conditions.

Marion Folster has a story typical of many of the Orcadian strawplaiters.

Marion Folster was born in 1835 to fisherman George Folster and Janet (Moar) in Birsay. By the 1841 census the family had grown to 5 children. George must have been doing well and in 1851 he was farming 2 acres of land and was a shoemaker. His son John also took up this trade. The family were living at Howquoy (also recorded as Hookquoy). The three girls in the family: Margaret age 25, Marion age 16 and Catherine age 14 were all earning money plaiting straw. It was usual for all the females in one family to be employed in this way.

George Folster continued to do well and his farm increased to 5 and then 8 acres. Janet died in 1869, aged 75. Marion and Catherine who were unmarried continued to live with their father. When George died in 1873, aged 75, the women moved to Ravy Hall, Birsay with their brother James who was a seafarer. Marion and Catherine were now employed as dressmakers. Perhaps there was a change in their fortunes for by the 1891 census they are recorded as general domestic servants. James was now retired and all three remained unmarried. James died in 1911 and the women continued to reside at Ravy Hall. Marion died on 23rd of July 1916 aged 81 with Catherine dying only a few weeks later on 6th of August 1916 aged 78. They are buried together in the Birsay cemetery.

Deerness

This was another parish where it was much depleted of young active males who had to seek employment elsewhere.

Rev James Smellie records that ships once used to collect men from the parish bound for the Davis Strait, Greenland or the fishing in Iceland:

"but since the burning in 1823 of Mr Scoresby's ship, 'The Fame of Hull', a name occurring in almost all scientific dissertations on the Arctic regions, no whale fishing vessel has been seen here; and by the

Iceland fishermen, it has been almost deserted since the last French war." [23]

The vessel 'Fame' was launched in India in 1786 and sold to Portuguese owners. She was captured by a French privateer and then recaptured by the Royal Navy in 1794. As a slave ship she made 3 trips sailing out of Liverpool, picking up hundreds of slaves from North West Africa and transporting them to the West Indies.

"From 1818 on she was a whaler in the Greenland whale fishery, sailing from Whitby and then Hull. She burnt in 1823 while outward bound on a whaling voyage." [24]

The Fame of Hull bound for Greenland was consumed by fire and burned at Deer Sound on 23rd April 1823. All the crew were saved.

The Deerness landowners were: the Earl of Zetland, Mr Balfour of Trenaby and Mr Groat of Newhall. There was one school run by the Society for Propagating Christian Knowledge.

In 1841 the population of Deerness was 772. There were 28 women employed as straw plaiters (just under 4% of the total population). The youngest was 14 years old Isabella Stove of Barebreck who was engaged in strawplaiting along with her mother and sister. The oldest was Jane Linklater, 50, of Jameshouse. Hemp spinning was done by many women in the parish and so there was no economic need for them to engage in the production of strawplait when they were fully employed processing Hemp.

By 1851 the population of Deerness had only slightly increased to 786 but those engaged in the plaiting of straw had dropped to 19, 17 of whom were single and 2, Barbara Linklater and Fanny McLeod, were widows. The youngest was May Stove of Lighthouse, aged 16 and the oldest Ann Cormack, 54 of Little Newark. The 1851 census records no hemp spinners in Deerness.

Life was extremely hard for any woman widowed. Fanny MacLeod's husband, James had been an agricultural labourer. When he died, Fanny (Frances Drever) had to support her children by plaiting straw. Her oldest son, James, was working as a labourer elsewhere in Deerness. Her youngest son, Robert, was recorded in the 1851 census, aged 15, as being a violinist and daughter Elizabeth, aged 12, as a scholar. In 1861 Frances, now 56, was living at Knowes next to her son James and his family. Daughter Elizabeth was single and employed as a white seam sewer. This was plain sewing, possibly of shirts, and many women in Orkney were employed in this work.

Eday and Faray

"The greatest part of Eday being covered with moss, presents a great obstacle to agricultural improvement" noted Rev Simpson. The 'moss' or peat was used as fuel, not just in Eday but transported to other islands "and some cargoes have been sent to the Frith of Forth within the last two years." [25]

The tenants of Eday had free use of the peats but the landowner made money estimated at £139.16s a year from the many people who travelled to Eday to purchase peat at six shillings a fathom.

The islands of Eday and Faray had a combined population of 1,011 in 1841. Eleven women (1% of the islanders) were engaged in strawplaiting. One woman, Mary Reid, was a straw bonnet maker. Mary's sister, Barbara Reid, who was 15 years old, was one of the youngest. The oldest was 50 year old Jennet Harcus.

By 1851 the population of the two islands was recorded as 1,016 and only one woman was now employed at straw plaiting. She was Ann Burges an unmarried 50 year old woman who lived at Roadside, Eday.

A school was established in Eday in 1827 by the Committee of the General Assembly for Promoting of Education in the Highlands and Islands of Scotland. Before the school was set up children had been taught by family members in their own homes mostly through reading religious texts.

"The Assembly's school however has been of great benefit to the parish, as it has spread education among all the families; taught the young to read with more accuracy than formerly, as well as taught them branches to which they could not have access before." [26]

The school was not free and fees of between 1/6 and 3/- were paid quarterly. In summer children were still needed for work on the farms and so attendance varied with the seasons: 24 in the summer, 36 in the winter.

Isabella Cormack was a young strawplaiter living at Black Banks Eday. Her father, Henry, was a farmer and brother Henry was a fisherman. Isabella and her older sister Barbara both earned an income plaiting straw. The family was a large one. It included their mother, also Isabella, and younger brother James. The family needed the support of the additional income. On 11th of March 1847, Isabella married John Eunson from Holm. He was employed in Eday as a teacher and whilst they were setting up their home at Sandhill with their little daughter, Isabella contributed to the family income as a seamstress. The family grew and prospered. By the 1861 census there are two more children: John and Robert. They could also now afford to have a servant.

Isabella and John moved with their family to Lanarkshire. John was now a school master and the job came with accommodation, the School House, Cadder. Their youngest son, John, continued to live with them and at 14 he was assisting his father in the school as a pupil teacher. After her husband's death, Isabella had to move out of the school house and went to live in Shields Road, Govan with her son John who was employed as a clerk in an iron foundry. Isabella died on 31st of October 1897, aged 72, in Glasgow.

Evie, Rendall and Gairsay

The main landowners of the area were William Traill of Woodwick, John Balfour and William Gordon. During the Napoleonic wars with France, Rev David Pitcairn records that many men in the area joined the army and 'especially the navy'. [27]

Interestingly in his statistical account of the parish, the Rev Pitcairn, records the illnesses and health condition of the people.

"Feverish colds, with dysentery, occur every season; cases of ague and consumption occur occasionally, and very few of the people who are advanced in life, are free from rheumatic attacks." This he puts down to the damp climate of the area. There are also '2 persons insane', '4 more or less fatuous' and '3 females are blind.' [28]

In 1841 the population of Evie and Rendall, including the island of Gairsay, was 1,518 with 16 women (1%) engaged at straw plaiting. Three of those women: Barbara Hourston, Betty Grieve and Ann Bichan all resided in Gairsay. Gairsay's population was 71 made up of 30 males and 41 females. Ann Bichan was also the oldest woman occupied in the trade at age 55 and there was no one under the age of 25 plaiting straw.

There was a parish school in Evie which was free. The teacher there gave £4 out of his £30 annual salary to employ a teacher in Gairsay. There were also several other non-parochial schools.

"All the people of the parish, of proper age, can read." [29]

By 1851 the population of the parishes of Evie and Rendall, including the island of Gairsay had dropped to 1,446 with 43 women (3%) now employed in straw plaiting, although none of those are now in Gairsay. The island's population had fallen to 41: 21 males and 20 females.

One of the youngest employed in Evie was 16 year old Ann Anderson of Indnagar. The widow, Christian Turnbull, 70, of Dyke, Evie may also have still been plaiting straw. The marital status of the women was: 37 single, 3 widows, and 3 married.

Strawplaiting was a way the women in the household could add extra income to the farm. Ann Calder and her two sisters, Phoebe and Betsy, did just that at their father's (John Calder) farm at Turndale/Turria Dale, Evie. It was an 11 acre property but when the strawplait trade collapsed, the daughters had to find other sources of employment. Christina Calder an older sister returned home and turned her skills to dressmaking. She married a ploughman David Leask. They continued to live with her father and Phoebe after her mother's death.

Betsy Calder went to work as a cook in the home of James Robertson, Sherriff Substitute of Orkney who lived in Albert Street, Kirkwall.

Ann Calder had a son, James Moar on 31st of March 1856. The young James continued to live at John Calder's farm. Ann went into domestic service on the 400 acre farm owned by George MacKenzie at Feolquoy. There she met ploughman James Offord and on April 18th 1861 they married. This relationship resulted in the birth of a daughter, Jane 1862. Ann was now again living with her father on his farm where she was to remain. After her father's death, Ann took on the working of the farm. James Moar became a fisherman. Jane and Ann's grandson, James Offord, were also being supported on the croft. It was the way that families cared for their relations. Ann's oldest sister, Jane, came to live out her last years at the small farm and James married. Ann's daughter Jane had secured employment as a domestic servant on the farm of Magnus Matches. On Ann's death Jane returned to her family home which she continued to farm with her son, James, a fisherman.

Ann Calder's first son, James Moar was to have a tragic death when he was drowned on 22nd of December 1916 aged 60. He had been sailing in a skiff with his friend, Robert Harper, from Kirkwall to his farm at Bught, Rendall. The empty boat was found the next day at Hacksness, Shapinsay with her sails set. The bodies of the men were not recovered. James left a widow and four children. [30]

Firth and Stenness

In 1841 the population of Firth and Stenness was 1,167 of which 23 women (2%) were employed plaiting straw and one women was a straw bonnet maker. One of the youngest was Margaret Louttit, 13, of Holland, Firth. The oldest was Elspet Scletter, 55, of Redland, Firth.

There were several women with the name 'Margaret Louttit', some with variations of the spelling of Louttit. Another Margaret Louttit lived at Breck, Stenness. Her father, Thomas died in 1841 at the age of 54. He was a farmer. On his death his widow, Christian/Christina continued to farm 4 acres until her death aged 79 in 1867. Her daughter Margaret and son Thomas, who at one point had been at sea, continued to live in the house after her death. Margaret was a shirt maker and knitter after the end of the strawplaiting industry. Thomas became a tailor. He predeceased Margaret, dying in 1873 aged 57. Margaret died in 1886 aged 69. All four are buried in Stenness Kirkyard.

"In memory of THOMAS LOUTTIT who died January 13th 1841 aged 54, CHRISTINA LEASK his wife died October 4th 1867 aged 79, THOMAS LOUTTIT their son died June 23rd 1873 aged 57, MARGARET LOUTTIT their daughter died June 10th 1886 aged 69. With Christ which is far better."

The 1842 Statistical Account records:

"Straw plaiting is performed by young girls in their father's houses. They are employed by Mr Ramsay in Kirkwall and Mr Heddle in Stromness". [31]

The main landowners in the area were Mrs Stewart, Burness; the Earl of Zetland; and James Baikie of Tankerness. There had not been many farming improvements and there was only a small amount of fishing done. That was for oysters in the Bay of Firth.

Both Firth and Stenness had parochial schools which were free. There was also one in each parish run by the Society for Propagating of Christian Knowledge.

By 1851 the population of the two parishes had increased to 1,326. There were 27 women (2%) now employed plaiting straw and one woman Mary Goudie, Sherounda, Stenness, was making straw bonnets. The youngest was Anne Gray, 18, Nether Bigswell, Stenness and the oldest was Catherine Jack, 69, Horraldshay, Firth. The marital status of the straw plaiters was 26 single and one widowed.

Anne Gray and her mother, who was unmarried, were both plaiting straw. Anne left the home to go into domestic service in Stromness. It was a live-in position with the family of draper James Garriock. Her mother stayed on at Nether Bigswell.

For women who remained single strawplaiting provided an essential income, even when the prices for their labour dropped. Margaret Yorston in Redland was plaiting straw throughout the time the industry was established in Orkney. She lived to be a great age but it was an extremely hard life, living on a low income. When the industry collapsed she became a pauper and ended her days as a lodger in the home of James Taylor at Nap House. She died on 1st of February 1872, at 80 years of age but possibly much older.

Harray

There were numerous landowners in Harray. The Rev Thomas Blyth in the Statistical Account suggests that there were 100 both residential and non-residential. This included the Earl of Zetland who was also the patron of Harray. The parish had two schools: 'The Society school and another which is conducted by a person entirely at his own adventure. About 130 children attend the schools and there are none under the age of fifteen who cannot read or write.' [32]

In 1841 the population of Harray was 772. 131 women (17%) were employed plaiting straw and an additional two women, Margaret Russland Skiirpaquoy, and Mary Kirkness, Moan, were making straw bonnets.

The youngest straw plaiter in Harray was 10 year old Jean Hourston who lived at London, Harray. The poverty was such at the time, even for those in work, that although her father Thomas worked as a labourer, her mother was registered as a pauper. Jean and her older sister Mary brought in that essential extra income with plaiting straw.

The oldest strawplaiter was Margaret Clouston, 60, of Nearhouse.

"Several of the manufacturers have agencies in Stromness and Kirkwall.. It is sent, when plaited, to Manchester or Liverpool." [33]

By 1851 the population of Harray had dropped to 750 with only 47 women (6%) now engaged with plaiting straw. Only one woman is recorded as making straw bonnets: Christian Flett, Lammaquoy.

The martial status of the women was as follows: 43 of the women were single, 4 married and 1 widowed.

Jessie (Janet) King's mother, Katherine Hourston, married William King in Stromness. The marriage certificate of the 15th November 1810 records him as a soldier in Captain McNeill's Company, 9th r.v battalion. Many soldiers were billeted in Orkney at this time both on their way to campaigns and preparing home defences. Jessie was born on 19th of May 1811. She ended up living with her two aunts in How o' Dilly, Harray. All three women were unmarried and whilst Jessie earned money as a strawplaiter her aunts, Margaret and Christian Hourston, were wool spinners and stocking knitters. After the deaths of her aunts, Jessie continued to live in the property earning income as firstly an egg gatherer then as a knitter. She died in her late seventies on 5th February 1897. She is buried in the graveyard at St Michael's Kirk, Harray with a simple inscription: "Jessie King who died 5th February 1897."

Holm and Paplay

The population of Holm and Paplay in 1841 was 866. There are no records of women engaged in strawplaiting.

The non-resident landowner was Alexander Graeme of Graemeshall who possessed nearly the whole of the parish. Most of the men were employed in farming but fishing for cod and herring took place in Holm Sound.

Alexander Graeme set about farm improvements and changing the tenantry terms. Tenant farmers were now offered 15 year leases with increases in rent after each 5 year period. Runrig was removed and the tenants had to put a certain proportion of their newly allotted fields to green crop and grass.

Flax had in the past been a very successful crop with many women employed in the spinning of it for the manufacture of linen. That industry had collapsed but hemp was grown and spun by some women in the parish.

Women employed at harvest time could earn between 14 and 18/- a week. A man could earn £1. 5/- a day for harvest work. Every farm would have access to a boat for fishing.

There was one parochial school which had been established for about 35 years. The Rev Andrew Smith records that from the age of 7 children would be employed during the spring, summer and autumn months, attending school during the winter when work could not be done outside.

From the age of 15 many of the young men would leave and never return.

"Most of the youth have no other means of living but as engaging as hands on board of coasting vessels and revenue cutters, or vessels trading to the Baltic and foreign countries, and few of them ever return." [34]

By 1851 the population had dropped to 749 with 6 (0.8%) women plaiting straw. The women were all single aged between 27 Barbara Dishon, Windwall and 58 Jean Sinclair, Cot of Brekquoy. Barbara Dishon's father had been a weaver. After his death she lived with her aunt who is listed as an 'inmate'. Barbara supported her aunt with an income from strawplaiting. After her aunt's death Barbara, now living alone, worked as a sewer. On her death in 1878 she was recorded as a domestic servant. This employment history: strawplaiting to sewing to domestic service, was a very common way for women – especially single women – to earn an income.

Hoy and Graemsay

There were 4 landowners: Robert Heddle, John Balfour, Rev G Hamilton and Harry Cruickshank. The Rev Hamilton records in the Statistical Accounts of the period that there is some herring fishing with the employment of 7 boats. There were, however, 3 schools serving the area.

In 1841 the population of the islands of Hoy (not including Walls) and Graemsay was 547. There were 16 women (3%) employed plaiting straw. One of the youngest was Jean Lyon, 14, of Clett, Graemsay, with the oldest being Ann Lyon, 55, recorded in the census as living in 'A Chamber'.

Jean Lyon's father was a fisherman. Jean married fisherman John Johnston in 1858. They had four of a family; Jean, Isaac, Catherine and James before John Johnston died. As a widow, Jean knitted stockings for extra income and eventually went to live with her unmarried sister, Ann, who also knitted stockings.

By 1851 the population had dropped to 615 and only 5 women (0.8%) continued to be employed plaiting straw. All the women lived in Graemsay. Of the 5 women, 3 are single and 2 are widows. Widow Margaret Yorston of Loan Lay Graemsay is also the oldest at 50 years of age.

Barbra Ritch married Charles Ritch a seafarer in 1841 and shortly after she gave birth to a son, Andrew. Barbra lived at Nether Corrigall, Graemsay with her baby son and was soon widowed. She earned an income firstly as a strawplaiter and when that industry collapsed, as a knitter mostly of stockings.

Kirkwall and St Ola

Kirkwall is described as being basically one long street by the Rev William Logie in his account of the town. On to these are many lanes but he adds that the new King Street which runs parallel has "several neat and commodious houses." People had gardens in which they grew a wide variety of fruits and berries: currants, gooseberries, strawberries, apples, pears, cherries and in one 'greenhouse' – grapes. [35]

The main landowners of Kirkwall and St Ola were: the Earl of Zetland, Mr Baikie of Tankerness, Mr Balfour of Trenaby, Mr Pollexfen of Cairston, Mr Laing of Papdale and Mr Graeme of Graemeshall.

St Magnus Cathedral dominated the town but the remains of the once great Kirkwall Castle were still to be found in what is now Castle Street. Although the town had seen a rapid growth in population up to this point there were now many empty properties and housebuilding had mostly stalled. Rev Logie puts this state of affairs down to the collapse of the kelp industry.

"The inhabitants of the town consist chiefly of shopkeepers, tradesmen of different crafts, sailors, boatmen and labourers. It also includes several custom and excise men; proprietors; 3 medical practitioners; 2 bankers; 6 men connected with the law; 5 Ministers and several school teachers." [36]

Kirkwall had an abundance of shops with nearly every second building selling a wide range of merchandise. Importing and exporting by ship from Kirkwall was very successful, however of the 68 vessels trading from the town only 21 were registered in Kirkwall. 47 of the vessels were registered in Stromness. There was a daily mail boat and steam ship sailings could convey passengers once a week to Leith, Edinburgh in around 40 hours.

The condition of the roads had also been improved which meant that the delivery of plaited straw from outwith the parish to the bonnet makers in Kirkwall was easier.

In 1841 the town of Kirkwall had a population of 3,581. There were 289 women (8%) employed plaiting straw. Catherine Corston, 55, Victoria Road was a straw plait dresser. Barbara James, 55, Victoria Street was a sizer of straw. Sibella Gray, 40, also of Victoria Street was a straw cleaner. Isabella Miller, 75, and Mary Gaudie, 65, both of Victoria Street were straw cutters. Barbara Maxwell, 65, Harbour Street was a straw oiler. William Bews, 20, of Catherine Place was a straw sorter. The population was made up of 1,508 males and 2,074 women. This means that 14% of women in the town were plaiting straw. The youngest was Isabella Bruce, age 9, of St Catherine's Place, and the oldest was 75 year old Catherine Wilson of Wellington Street.

Isabella Bruce lived in a house occupied by eleven other people: adults and children. These included her two siblings Anne, aged 7, and Betsy, aged 4. Multiple house occupancy was common and child labour provided an income for struggling families. Another Kirkwall street where many strawplaiters lived and worked was Wellington Street. Barbara MacKay, aged 15, lived in a household with ten others, four of whom were also strawplaiters.

The women who went into domestic service were paid £3 per annum. The plaiting of straw for hats and bonnets "occupies three fourths of the female population" [37]

"This manufacture has been carried on for forty years, and has proved a very seasonable source of emolument to the poorer classes.... In this manufacture, a woman earns from 3d to 9d per day, according to her skill and diligence or the time which she devotes to the employment." [38]

Kirkwall Grammar School had been established for hundreds of years and was referred to in the 15thC town's charter. An endowment from John Balfour of Trenaby ensured that 8 poor children received education at the Grammar school. There were about 80 to 100 pupils who paid a fee to attend. It included boys and girls. Their lessons consisted of, Latin, Greek, French, English, Mathematics, Navigation, Arithmetic and 'the principles of the Christian religion'.[39]

There was also a school run by the Society for the Propagating of Christian Knowledge attended by between 50 to 60 poorer children. There was a variety of privately run smaller schools. These included a school for young ladies, a charity school for girls funded by women, 3 Sabbath schools and an Infant school.

"The benefits of education are generally appreciated by parents; and there are scarcely any betwixt the ages of six and sixty who cannot read." [40]

There were also two libraries in the town, one of which, the Orkney Library, is still in operation today.

By 1851 the town of Kirkwall had increased to 3,869. Only 122 women (3%) were now employed straw plaiting. Robina Linnay, 59, of Queen Street, was a straw splitter. She resided in the house of manufacturer David Ramsay. Janet Millar, 75, also of Queen Street, was a retired straw cutter and Marion Gaudie, 74, of Victoria Street, was a straw sliverer. Of the 2,203 (57%) women in the population, the percentage plaiting straw had dropped to 6%. The youngest was Jane Sinclair, 7, of Victoria Street, and one of the oldest was Magadeline Bews, 73, of the High Street. The marital status of the women was: 95 single, 5 married and 25 widowed.

By 1851 many of the women who had made the fortunes for the merchants through strawplaiting were now registered as paupers. Sisters Catharine and Janet Flett, strawplaiters lived in Victoria Street and were very poor. Janet died in 1853:

"Janet Flett, unmarried poor, died 1st & was buried 4th July 1853." [41]

Catharine continued to live on in the Victoria Street home for a few more years.

Orphir and Cava

In 1841 the population of Orphir including the island of Cava was 1,064. There were 68 women (6%) employed as straw plaiters. There were 23 islanders living in Cava but none of them were engaged in the industry. When counting only the female population out of the 585, 11.6% were straw plaiters. The youngest employed was Williamina Moncrieff, aged 13, and the oldest was Cecilia Hay, aged 75.

Williamina married mason John Groundwater in 1848. Together they lived at Scorradale, Orphir with their young family. They had a good life together although beset by the tragedies of that time of two of their children dying in infancy and one son at the age of 19. Williamina outlived John by about 19 years and died in January 1918 at the age of 90.

By 1851 the population of the parish had risen to 1,157. There were 22 women (2%) employed plaiting straw. Out of the 639 women who lived in the parish 3.4% were engaged in the industry. All of the women were single.

Christian Ballentine of Bare Brecks, Orphir, was typical of most of the women becoming a stocking knitter with the ending of the strawplaiting industry. In her later years she was in receipt of a small pension.

Three sisters, Christian, Hellen and Phoebe Corner, were all helping to support their widowed mother at 'Aikiley' Orphir by plaiting straw. Phoebe married Alexander Groundwater in 1844, tragically dying just two years later. Hellen married Joshua Hay in 1845. She died in 1875 aged 60 after several years of illness. Christian, remained single all her life. After the collapse of strawplaiting she earned money as a stocking knitter and lived with her young niece Phoebe Groundwater who was a muslin veiner. Phoebe died when she was 18 having suffered from a continuous fever for 25 days. Christian continued to support herself but in her later years was said to have gone 'insane'. She died in 1896 aged 83 from a tumour on her liver which had resulted in jaundice.

North Ronaldsay

In 1841 the population of the island was 481 and in 1851 it had risen to 526. There is no record of strawplaiting taking place.

Rousay, Egilsay and Wyre (including Eynhallow)

In 1841 the total population for the four islands was 1,288. It is broken down into Rousay: 976; Egilsay: 190; Wyre: 96; and Eynhallow: 26. There were 28 women (2%) working as straw plaiters in Rousay and Egilsay. Of the 539 women in Rousay, there were 19 (3.5%) straw plaiting. Of the 107 women in Egilsay, 7 (6.5%) were straw plaiting. The youngest was 10 year old Francis Craigie, Egilsay, and the oldest was 55 year old Barbary Craigie, Rousay. Julia Mainland, 25, Nethermill, Rousay, was a bonnet maker.

Francis Craigie's father was a fisherman. She was plaiting straw from her childhood for more than 10 years. At the age of 10 she was living with Catherine Foulis, also a strawplaiter at Netherskail, Egilsay. Catherine never married and became a pauper when the industry collapsed earning some money spinning wool and living into her eighties.

By 1851 the population of the islands had decreased to 1,215. Only 14 women (1%)were now plaiting straw and the widow, Margaret Marwick, 29, Hullion, Rousay is making straw bonnets. 5 (1%) of the women straw plaiters are in Rousay out of a total female population there of 501. The rest, 9 (9%) are in Egilsay out of a female population there of 101. The youngest worker was Isabella Johnston, 17, Whitlet, Egislay. The oldest was in Egilsay, 60 year old, Catherine Fowlis, at Nether Skaill. One woman, Isabella Bews, Midskaill, Egilsay was married. The others were all single.

Isabella was married to farmer Hugh Bews on 14th of February 1851 but at the start of the marriage, possibly whilst pregnant, she resided with her parents, James and Isabella Mainland (née Bews) at Midskail Egilsay on their farm. It was while she was there that she was plaiting straw. Hugh and Isabella farmed 70 acres at Meanais, Egilsay with their growing family of children and grandchildren.

St Andrews

In 1841 the population of St Andrews was 921. 27 women (3%) were strawplaiters. Of the total number of women, 491, 5.5% were engaged in the industry. One of the youngest straw plaiters was 15 year old Betsy Delday of Lochend. The oldest was Margaret Esson, 65 of Little Grind.

Betsy Delday and her mother, Jean, living at Loch End, St Andrews, were both scraping out a living plaiting straw. As a widow, Jean had few sources of income and both women died as paupers, Betsy at the age of 43 in 1867, cause unknown. Jean died two years later aged 87 of 'old age'.

By 1851 the population in the parish was 926. Only 15 women (1.6%) were engaged in plaiting straw. There was a total of 441 women in St Andrews with 3.4% engaged in the industry. All the women were single except for one widow, Barbara Craigie of Heatherhouse. The youngest worker was Janet Dishon, 16, Kerrabreck and the oldest was Christian Garrioch, 55, now living at Lochend.

Christian Garrioch had plaited straw for many years and as an unmarried woman she took in her nephew, William Louttit, for a short period whilst he was an apprentice carpenter to a boat builder. Christian died a pauper, aged 66 in 1861 of an illness registered as 'a decay of nature' which she had suffered from for 3 months. William had taken her to live at his farm in her final months. He was now a successful carpenter and farmer. He was present at her death in his family home at 'Woodstock', Holm.

Sanday

In 1841 the population of Sanday was 1,892. There were 13 women (0.6%) plaiting straw. One woman, Jean Brock, 15, Storehouse, Cross, was making straw bonnets. One of the youngest workers was Betsy Muir, 25, Gateside Houses, Burness. She lived with her aunt Isabella Muir and her mother and all three were plaiting straw. After the death of her mother, Betsy continued to live with her aunt and her sister, Jean. They all worked at a variety of jobs, farm work, domestic service and for a time Betsy was sewing. Both Jean and Betsy died as paupers. Betsy died in 1864 aged 58 of a 'disease of the stomach' which she had suffered from for 18 years. Her devoted sister, Jean died in 1879 aged 70 of 'old age'. The deaths of both sisters were discovered by their neighbours.

By 1851 the population of Sanday had increased to 2,005 but only 6 women (0.3%) were strawplaiting and 3 were making straw bonnets: Janet Dearness, 50, Myrtlehall, Lady; Barbara Scott, 40, Schoolhouse, Cross; and Isabella Flett, 18 Towerhill, Burness. There was a total of 1,050 women in Sanday with 0.6% working plaiting straw. Three of the straw plaiters were single, 2 were widows and 1 was married. The widow Barbara Sinclair, Windaway, Cross, was also the oldest at age 55. The youngest was her daughter, also Barbara, living at the same address, aged 19. Both women had to find other paid work when strawplaiting ceased and that was in farm work. It was low paid, hard physical labour and a poor existence with both of them ending long but poverty laden lives as paupers. The elder Barbara Sinclair died aged 89 on 18th of February 1883. Her daughter, who remained single, died aged 84 on 5th of May 1916.

Sandwick

In 1821, 69 straw plaiters were recorded as living in Sandwick. One of the youngest was 12 year old Isabella Harvey, who lived at Skithva with her two sisters. Elizabeth her older sister aged 14 was also plaiting straw. The oldest strawplaiter recorded in this account for Sandwick was Jannet Tours, 57, of Mire Housegarth.

"The principle branch of manufacture carried on here is straw plaiting, which occupies almost all our younger females; or, in summer, reaping and preparing the 9 acres of rye that furnish the materials. The seeds are sown thick, that the straw may be long and fine. The stems are cut down before the grain ripens, tied near the lower end into very small bundles, steeped in boiling water for an hour, spread on the ground to bleach, and carted to the manufacturers house, where the upper part between the highest joint and the grain, which only in general is used, is pulled out; cut to a proper length, sifted or sorted to different degrees of fineness, and made up into small bundles, which are distributed to the girls who take them to their own houses to be plaited; they are paid according to the fineness of the straw, and excellence of the work." [42]

"The plaiters can earn 6d a day at the present rate of wages. The plaits are next washed, smoked, milled, and lastly put into the hands of other girls, who sew them together into bonnets. At one time, this manufacture was conducted in a very objectionable manner, by collecting numbers of young people in confined apartments, where as "evil communications corrupt good manners" and "one sinner destroyeth much good", it is to be feared the contaminated atmosphere was not only destructive to their bodily health, but to their moral purity. The same objections, however, do not apply to it as conducted at present in their own homes, where it has a tendency to introduce neatness and cleanliness; but it is a serious objection, that the whim of a London lady may render it unfashionable to appear under a thatch of straw, and thus at once throw destitute 3,000 Orcadian damsels." [42]

In 1841 the population of Sandwick was 1,033. There were 93 (9%) women working as straw plaiters. There was a total of 563 females with 16.5% engaged in the industry. The youngest was Mary Garson, 11, Scaebrae, and one of the oldest was Marjory Brass, 55, Croval.

Mary Garson's father, George, was a tailor. Mary, her sister, Margaret and her aunt, Ann Kirkness, were all engaged plaiting straw. On the death of her father all three women went to live with Mary's brother, also George, a stonemason. The women continued to earn money by plaiting straw. With the ending of the industry, like thousands of other unmarried women in Orkney, they were employed knitting, mostly stockings. George farmed at Newhall and Mary supported

the family by working on the farm. She died there on 11th of
October 1875, aged 45. She was covered in abscesses.
Margaret Garson predeceased Mary. She died on 3rd of April 1863,
aged 47, of 'a general weakening'.

By 1851 the population had increased to 1,100. Only 56 (5%) were
engaged in straw plaiting and one woman Sibella Brown,23, of
Hammerclett, was making straw bonnets. Ann Wishart, 50,
Howaback, was a retired straw cutter. Out of the total female
population of 608, 9% were straw plaiters. The youngest was Jane
Brass, 15, Whetherstown, and the oldest was Mary Stockan, 72, of
Quoyloo who had been a farm servant and plaiter of straw. Looking
at their marital status, 54 were single, 1 married and 2 widowed.

Janet Twatt of Vetquoy, Sandwick, had been a strawplaiter for the
whole of the time the industry was in Orkney. At the collapse of
strawplaiting she found employment knitting stockings which she
did with her niece, Betsy. Janet died after several years of illness on
2nd of April 1866 aged 64. She had never married.

Shapinsay

In 1841 the population of the island of Shapinsay was 929. There
were 32 women engaged in straw plaiting and one, Elizabeth
Hutchison, 35, Guibro, listed as a 'straw maker'. Out of the total
population of the island, 3.4% of women were engaged in the
industry. Out of the female only population of 489 it accounts for
6.5% of employment.

Isabella Brodie had married George Hume a tailor on 17th of March
1825 in Shapinsay. Sadly George died just two years later at the age
of 28. Isabella never remarried and earned an income plaiting straw.

She died of 'unknown causes' on 25th of August 1859 aged 59.

By 1851 Shapinsay's population had fallen to 898 and there were only 7 (0.7%) women working as straw plaiters, or 1.5% of the female population of 466. Of the 7 women: 5 were single, 1 widowed and 1 married. The latter was Margaret Sketheway, Canada, who was also the oldest at 66 years of age. The youngest was 24 year old Mary Stevenson of Waterhouse. Mary Stevenson's father died in 1847. Mary provided an income for herself and her mother, Elispeth by plaiting straw.

Margaret Sketheway and the other two oldest women, the widow Sibella Inkster, 57, and Mary Work, 56, were not born in Shapinsay. Margaret and Mary were both from Egilsay. Sibella was from the parish of St Andrews. Margaret Sketheway was married to James, a farm labourer and she supplemented the household income where her sons, William and James were fishermen. James died in 1852 aged 75. Margaret lived until she was 79 and died on 22nd August 1862 of 'unknown causes'.

South Ronaldsay and Burray

In 1841 the total population for the islands of South Ronaldsay, Burray, Swona and Pentland Skerry totalled 3,174.

- South Ronaldsay: 1,847
- Burray: 1,262
- Swona: 54
- Pentland Skerry: 11

All of the women involved in strawplaiting lived in South Ronaldsay. 4 bonnet makers also lived in the island. Out of the total population of South Ronaldsay, 73 (4%) women were plaiting straw. Of the 958 women on the island, 7.6% are strawplaiters.

Catherine and Isabella Gutcher of Gaira St Mary's were both strawplaiters. They lived with their widowed mother who ran the farm. Their two brothers were fishermen.

By 1851 the population of the islands had dropped to 3,086. Only one woman, Margaret Swan, 23, Swan House, St Peters is plaiting straw. There were 3 women making straw bonnets. All the women lived in St Peters. Margaret Swan lived with her widowed mother, a knitter of stockings, her sister Ann and two children at Swan House.

Stromness

The 1821 census for Stromness records 271 straw plaiters, 1 straw cutter, 1 bonnet maker and 8 manufacturers. One of the youngest strawplaiters was 10 year old Margaret Archibald with the oldest, Margaret Inkster, 45. The straw cutter was a man, John Clouston, 53.

The 1841 population of Stromness was 2,784. There were 5 manufacturers, 8 bonnet makers, 1 sorter of straw, 1 straw maker and 302 strawplaiters (11% of the total population). Of the 1,690, females in Stromness, 18% were employed plaiting straw.

The two youngest workers were 6 year olds, Elizabeth Spence and Isabella Tait who both lived in Queen Street. Elizabeth Spence, her sister Anne aged 8 and their mother, also Elizabeth, all plaited straw to support the family income. Elizabeth's father was a farm labourer. The oldest strawplaiter in Stromness was Margary Sinclair, 65, of Main Street who lived there with her twenty year old daughter, supporting them both on her income.

"There are a few straw plait manufacturers, who employ a number of women in the town as well as in the country. This manufacture has been, for some time past, upon the decline; and being at all times dependent upon the caprice of fashion, has lately afforded a scanty subsistence to the many young females who totally depend upon it for their support. They are now allowed to plait in their own homes, which has been found more conducive to their health and morals, than doing so collectively, in the houses of the manufacturers, which was the original custom." [43]

Although they are long demolished, a row of cottages existed in Queen Street, Stromness and by 1968 they were still there but much dilapidated. One or two in the 1960s continued to be occupied and the last one with a roof was used as a trout hatchery.

It is part of the folk history of the town that soldiers were billeted in the cottages at the end of the Napoleonic Wars. The Queen Street cottages were filled with young women, employed at plaiting straw, and it is suggested that the name of the street derives from the word 'Quean' meaning a young girl.

A closer look at some of the families bears this out.

John Murray, an army pensioner, lived in the cottages and married a local woman. Three of his daughters were employed plaiting straw, Janet, Margaret and Isabella. In 1838 Janet gave birth to a son William. She was unmarried. William's father, George Moar, was a seaman. Janet's sister, Isabella, married sailor John Smith and their surviving son, Thomas, also went to the sea. He ended up staying with Janet and Margaret, his two maiden aunts, who were now getting by as knitters.

This was all fairly typical of a busy port. Young men were often away for long periods of time working out at sea, in the army, or for the Hudson Bay company. Families supported one another with relatives taking care of one another when the need arose.

Catherine Tait was married to a fisherman. All the women in the family were employed plaiting straw, daughter Catherine, 15, Jane, also possibly 15 and Isabella, 6. The young boys of the family were not so employed.

The Baikie's was another household where all the women were plaiting straw whilst their brother William was a fisherman. He married Mary Anderson, a strawplaiter, who also lived in the row of cottages. This was the way it was. A close knit community supporting one another. Mary died young and eventually William returned to living with an unmarried sister, Anne, who earned some money knitting stockings.

By 1851 the population of Stromness had slightly decreased to 2,753. The number of manufacturers remained at 5 but there were now 17 bonnet makers recorded. 105 (4.8%) women were engaged plaiting straw. The number of females residing in Stromness at this time was 1,672, of those 6% were strawplaiters.

One of the youngest was Catherine Irvine, 15, Old Queena, Redland Hill, and the oldest was widow 62 year old May Firth, Queen Street. There were 92 of the women single, 6 married and 7 widows.

The women in Catherine Irvine's family were all experienced strawplaiters. Catherine's father, Edward, who was a farmer, died in 1863 aged 80 years of 'old age'. Her mother, Ann (Yorston) died in 1867 aged 74, also of what was then described as 'old age'.

Catherine continued to live on at Queena with two of her sisters who were all now engaged working the farm and knitting. When her sister Isabella died, Catherine and Susan remained at Queena carrying on the work of the farm and knitting. Susan died in 1905 aged 82 of 'senile decay'. What of Catherine? Well it appears she married, William Spence, a farm labourer, on 25th of February 1897. According to the records William Spence was 48 and Catherine, 63.

Stronsay

In 1841 the population of Stronsay was 1,254. There were 16 straw plaiters and 1 woman, Mary Kirk, 25, of Dirdal, Lady Kirk, making straw bonnets. One of the youngest straw plaiters was 15 year old Margaret Miller of Hilly House, St Peters, and the oldest was Catherine Devine, 65, of Clyth, Lady Kirk.

By 1851 the population of Stronsay had dropped to 1,211. Only 10 women were now strawplaiting and they were all unmarried. The youngest was Hellen Cooper, 20, Braehead, and the oldest Mary Elphinstone, 64, Bombasty. Hellen Cooper lived mostly with her mother and father who was an agricultural labourer. At the collapse of the strawplaiting industry Hellen went into domestic service.

Mary Chalmers was born in 1816, her father, Peter, was an agricultural labourer and fisherman. Those were the most common occupations for men in Stronsay in this period. Fishing was an extremely dangerous occupation. Mary married Peter Peace, a fisherman in 1842. By the 1861 census, Mary was a widow, living with her daughter, Peterina, who was the school mistress at the New School. Mary was earning an income by sewing shirts.

Most of the women were either single or widows. Sisters Mary and Barbara Elphinstone who lived at Bombasty, Lady Kirk, were paupers.

"They receive from 1s. to 15s. during the year. The only fund for relief of the poor is that which is procured by weekly collections in the parish churches on Sabbath, with the exception of a donation of £2. 2s. per annum from Mr Balfour of Trenaby for the poor of Stronsay." [44]

Strawplaiter Margaret Sinclair of Midgarth, St Peters had married a carpenter. She was widowed in May 1841 when James died at the age of 29. Margaret lived till 1890 but had to rely on living for a few years with her daughter, Jemima, married to farmer John Gorie. She is buried in St Peters graveyard.

Barbara Scott who lived with her brother, Robert, and mother at Wardhill, St Peters, was to remain single. Robert was a carpenter, a trade at which he excelled. Barbara is recorded in every census until her death in 1891 as single. There is, however, an inscription on a gravestone in Bay Cemetery which says the following:

"In memory of JAMES WATERS, Boston, Mass. USA who died 26-11-1912 aged 72 years, his mother BARBARA SCOTT, Wardhill who died 4-5-1891 aged 74 years, his grandmother MARY SHEARER who died 22-2-1854, MARGARET MEIL SCOTT who died 14-8-1935 aged 65, JOHN WILSON SCOTT, Wardhill who died 16-2-1939 aged 70 years."

The 1851 census records James Walters, age 9, living with the family at Wardhill. Is this the same James remembered on the inscription 'Waters' or 'Walters'? The spelling of names is inconsistent over this whole period.

Walls, Flotta and Faray

The 1841 population for the islands of Walls and Flotta was 1,614. This was made up of Walls (1,209) Flotta and Faray (405). There were no women on the two islands recorded as plaiting straw. One woman, Susan Wilson, 25, of Wing, Walls, was making straw bonnets.

"Straw plaiting is also carried on to a considerable extent by the women". [45]

This is a frequent inconsistency which occurs in the records. It could be that by 1841 Rev Weir's records of employment in the islands were out of date.

By 1851 the population of Walls had increased slightly to 226. That of Flotta and Faray had increased to 441. There were no women engaged in either straw plaiting or the making of straw bonnets.

Westray and Papa Westray

In 1841 the population of the two islands of Westray and Papa Westray totalled 2,131. It was made up of Westray (1,794) and Papa Westray (337). There were 8 women plaiting straw and all live in Westray. One of the youngest was Jean Reid, 15, Cage in the North Parish. Jean and her sister, Margaret, aged 20, were both plaiting straw to support the rest of the all female household. The oldest was Isabella Grey, 55, Brugh, also in North Parish. Her income from strawplaiting was helping to support Thomas Meil recorded as an 'indigent' which means he was poor.

"Straw plaiting was, for some years, among the females of this parish, a very general manufacture; but the very little encouragement now held out has nearly put a stop to this work." [46]

By 1851 the population of the two islands had increased to 2,459. This was made up of Westray (2,088) and Papa Westray (371). There are no records of women straw plaiting by this time.

The Bonnet Makers

The plaited straw was transported to the women who would sew it together to make the bonnets. This work was extremely skilled as it required fine needlework. The bonnets would also be finished off with various decorations such as ribbons. Between 1841 and 1851 there are recorded just under 100 bonnet makers in Orkney. Most of the women live in the towns of Kirkwall and Stromness but some are living in rural and island areas.

The 1841 census records the following bonnet makers outwith the two main towns:

Mary Reid, 20, Banke, Eday

Isabella Harray, 20, Horraldshay, Firth

Mary Kirkness, 25, Moan and Margaret Russland, 30 Skirrpaquoy, Harray

Julia Mainland, 25, Nethermill, Rousay

Jean Brock, 15, Storehouse, Cross, Sanday

Mary Ross, 30, St Margaret's Hope and Ann Ross, 35, Grimness, St Peter's, South Ronaldsay. Also in the same island are two women recorded as 'milliner' which may mean they also make straw bonnets. Mary Russland, 20 and her sister Jessie, 15, Coolack, St Peter's.

Mary Chalmers, 25, Dirdal, Lady Kirk, Stronsay

Susan Wilson, 25, Wing, Walls

The 1851 census records the following bonnet makers outwith the two main towns:

Margaret Stanger, 32, Bowan, Birsay

Mary Goudie, 19, Sherouda, Stenness

Margaret Smith,39, Nisthouse, is listed as 'formerly straw hat maker' and Christian Flett,69, Lammaquoy, are both in Harray. Margaret Smith is not recorded as a straw hat maker in the previous census so perhaps she was only making the bonnets for a short time.

Margaret Marwick, 29, Hullion, Rousay

Janet Dearness, 50, Myrtlehall, Barbara Scott, 40, Schoolhouse, Cross and Isabella Flett,18 Towerhill, Burness, are all in Sanday. Isabella is also a dressmaker.

Sibella Brown, 23, Hammerclett, Sandwick

Betsty Stewart, 26, Smith House, Mina Harrold, Cletts and Mary Ross, 43, are in St Peter's South Ronaldsay.

All of these women are single. Margaret Marwick of Rousay is a widow.

The nature of the industry meant that most of the bonnet makers resided in Stromness and Kirkwall which both had thriving ports.

Bonnet Makers	Stromness	Kirkwall
• 1841 Census:	8	33
• 1851 Census:	16	18

All of the women were single with the following exceptions:
Three are widows: Helen Finlayson, 28, Main Street, Stromness, and in Kirkwall: Betsy Slater, 45, Palace Street; and Barbara Gorie, 57, Victoria Street.

Three are married: Elizabeth Marwick, 22, Tait's Close, and Christina Sutherland, 32, Pump Well Road, Stromness; and Jane Shearer, 24, Albert Lane, Kirkwall.

A full list of all those recorded in working in the strawplaiting industry is included in the additional notes.

Straw plait display in Orkney Museum, Kirkwall.

The Manufacturers

The term 'Manufacturers' described those who purchased the plait and the straw bonnets to be traded onwards. There are some women recorded in census returns as being 'manufacturers'. Were these women also exporting the product via the shipping lines or were they another layer in the industry? Could they have been a middle person who some of the merchants in straw plait used liaising between the plait and bonnet makers?

In the 1841 census the following women are recorded as 'straw plait manufacturer':

Mary Mowat, Victoria Street, Kirkwall and Cicla Sutherland, Gray's Buildings, Stromness.

In the 1841 census, two women, Ann Hourston and Betty Robertson, of North End Rendall, are described as 'manufacturer of plaits'.

In the 1851 census Catherine Tait is described as 'visitor, straw manufacturer', Queen Street, Stromness.

This is where the words used by the census recorder, or what the individual being recorded describes themselves as, is open to some interpretation.

The control of shipping is crucial in making a judgment in this because that was a male dominated business. It was shipping and the onward trade connections that were vital in conducting the business of strawplait. It is unlikely that women in Orkney were involved at this level of the trade and were not 'manufacturers' in the same sense as the male merchants were.

The men whose business it was to trade in strawplait used the ports of either Stromness or Kirkwall. For some, fortunes were made, but not for all. It was a risky business because many things could go awry in the complex supply chain which had rapidly grown up.

The Kirkwall Merchants

Rev David Ramsay

The Rev David Ramsay was to become one of the most important traders in Kirkwall but David Ramsay was not from Orkney. What brought him to the islands in the early years of the 19th century and what drove his success?

David Ramsay was born in 1781 in Barry, Forfarshire (today Angus), where nearly every household wove cloth for onward transport to Dundee and export abroad. Ramsay, himself, was trained in weaving cloth. Most people in the town belonged to the Established Church of Scotland but not David Ramsay. He was inspired by the teachings of the preachers Rowland Hill and Robert and James Haldane. David Ramsay became a Dissenter.

In 1807 he travelled to Orkney as a minister in the Congregationalists and as the 'new' church was just getting going he took no money for his ministry but funded his life by his own means – as a trader in strawplait.

The strawplaiting and bonnet making industry was just taking off in Orkney where he was introduced to the trade by James Borwick who was to become his very good friend. David Ramsay, being there at the start, carried on with the trade throughout its boom years.

Much of the strawplait used by Ramsay's plaiters was grown on the farms of Seatter, Cleat and Holland, on the east side of Kirkwall. Demand was so great in those early years that many other merchants and traders fastened onto it as a quick money earner. This meant that when the harvest was not enough to meet the demand that the raw materials had to be imported too.

Kirkwall was growing fast. As Ramsay's income grew he purchased a plot of land, part of Millers Park, the Lands of Papdale on April 22nd 1829. He built a fine house with a garden in what became known as Queen Street. The house and that adjoining it, recently renovated, is now occupied by Business Gateway.

In 1867 the buildings were put up for sale by the Trustees of Ramsay's estate. The sale by public auction described it as:

"a large and commodious dwelling house with garden, stable, washing house and other outhouse and conveniences attached, at present possessed by Mr David Bruce, and the small self-contained dwelling house immediately adjoining it possessed by Capt R Heddle – posted by Alexander Bain." [47]

It is said that opposite the house was a public watering source which was known as 'Ramsay's Well'.

Ramsay married Margaret Bews from Kirkwall and produced a large family: William, Elizabeth, Isabella, John, David and Margaret. James went to sea and John became a cabinet maker but the rest of the family were employed assisting their father in the straw plait industry. The household was a large one with a live-in servant and a lodger who was employed as a straw splitter.

63

"The introduction of the straw splitter made it possible to split straws into equal-sized splints that were easier to plait into good quality, narrow plaits. By about 1815 the price of a splitter had fallen to around 6d, so it was affordable and a woman could use it to increase her income to possibly £1 a week, maybe double or more than the wage of an agricultural labourer." [48]

The industry was so massive and in those early boom years so 'manic' with thousands of women employed that there were often disputes between the various dealers over plait. The plait was being processed not just in Stromness and Kirkwall but in many parishes. It then had to be sent to the traders who would sell it onwards and export it from Orkney. It was all part of a distribution chain linking up the processing and plaiting of the straw to make bonnets. Just like today when a parcel is delivered to the wrong address that also happened in 19th century Orkney.

David Ramsay got into a dispute with another trader, John Taylor of Kirkwall, over wrongly delivered plaits. John Taylor accused Ramsay of receiving and keeping for himself plaits bought by Taylor. In a letter from David Ramsay to John Taylor dated 20th July 1813, Ramsay tried to take the heat out of the argument by offering to give Taylor some plaits. David Ramsay says:

"Mid June you called with 3 plaits at my house saying that I received 5 of yours. They are mine but I said I would give you 5 and pay for them being plaited by Cuper…I am willing to give you the profits on the 5 plaits with certain conditions."[49]

And we get an indication that this was not an unusual problem as the letter confirmed that Ramsay had a similar wrong delivery previously but had settled it with the trader concerned, Oliver Scott, amicably.

Ramsay paid the women plaiters and processors money,

"to all who wished it on the return of their work, but many who preferred their money to lie in Mr Ramsay's hands received a ticket with the amount due to them, to be drawn at their convenience."[50]

The various Orkney traders had their own connections south for the plaited straw. David Ramsay exported his to the firm of J and A Muir in Greenock.

The most important aspect of David Ramsay's life was his Ministry.

"The Rev Mr Ramsay was a splendid Minister who occupied the church now known as The Temperance Hall, and which belongs to The Good Templars. He preached three sermons every sabbath." [51]

David Ramsay died on the 2nd August 1853. An Inventory [52] recorded on 28th February 1854 of his effects is as follows:

- Value of household furniture and other effects
      £42 9 /- 6d
- Debt due by Wm Frear (flesher) £3 1/- 10d
- Principal sum due by the trustees of Mill Street Chapel
      £70 plus interest £2 12/- 2d total £72 12/- 2d
- Sum contained in deposit receipt to the National Bank
      of Scotland's branch at Kirkwall £200 plus
      interest £1 11/- 6 d Total £201 11/- 6d
- Balance of account due by Messrs Muir Connel (?) and
      Brodie of Glasgow £43 13/- 6d
- **Total = £363 8/- 6d**

The Trustees : Peter Cursiter, William Mainland (both merchants) and Richard Spence joiner, took care of the property at Queen Street.

David Ramsay's grave in St Magnus Cathedral Kirkwall is a very modest stone which was put in place by his congregation. As such there is no mention of his family on it and it is in a poor state.

"[Flat or fallen stone] In memory of Revd DAVID RAMSAY, for many years Minister of the Congregational Church Kirkwall, who died on 2nd Aug 1855 aged 75. Also of Rev JAMES MCNAUGHTON, 7 years Minister of the same Church, who died on the 10th Dec 1859 aged 40. This stone is erected by members of the Congregational Church of Kirkwall as a memorial of their love and esteem toward these servants of Jesus Christ. Also Rev J W CHALMERS, one year Minister of the above Church, died 3rd June 1895 aged 39 years. With Christ in Glory."

For such a man, dedicated to his religious beliefs, and so hard working, for him, what was important was the church he was instrumental in developing.

"Mr Ramsay was an earnest man, gifted, full of humour, who, as used to be said about him, "thought for himself about everything." And whose adherence to Independency in early life had offended his relatives, and seriously injured his own worldly prospects." [53]

George and James McBeath

George McBeath [or MacBeath] (1800 -1847) was a successful merchant whose life spanned the years of straw plait manufacture in Orkney. In 1828 George married Isabella Mainland.

Shipping was crucial in the supply and distribution chain of the straw plait industry.

In 1839 George McBeath was involved in a long running dispute over the schooner, Eclipse. The Eclipse was originally purchased by four men with equal shares in the ship. George McBeath bought out his partners with the exception of one, Patrick Gorie.

The case for McBeath was that he owned the majority of the shares in the Eclipse and he wanted access to the books and accounts of the vessel.

Defending the action was Patrick Gorie and Andrew Louttit, shipping agents and merchants of Kirkwall. Andrew Louttit had been appointed the ship's husband by all the original shareholders. He had possession of the books, papers and accounts of the vessel. McBeath, as the largest shareholder, wanted rid of Louttit and possession of the books.

Gorie and Louttit refused to hand over the books. In addition to this George McBeath wanted payment from Gorie of £5 sterling.

The case went on for some time with Patrick Gorie throwing doubt on McBeath's competence at managing the vessel. George McBeath replied to this that the ship's husband is not in day to day management – that is the job of the ship's master. He reaffirmed his claim in being the majority shareholder, questioning why should he pay for the services of Louttit when he could do that job himself. George Mcbeath won the case. [54]

This was the kind of tough negotiating that went on over shipping, which was vital for Orkney's imports and exports.

George McBeath was also Treasurer of the Benevolent Society of Orkney. The Benevolent Society of Orkney loaned money with interest and when the debt was not repaid it would claim the lands and rentals due. James Stewart had borrowed £1,200 sterling plus interest from the Society and put up as collateral his lands in Rousay, Rosiebank and St Ola.

In 1838 money which had been borrowed from the Society by James Stewart had not been repaid and to recover the debt on his death a list of tenants (on land once owned by Stewart) on Rousay were served with notices for rent arrears. [55]

1. William Seatter tenant Saviskaill
2. Magnus Clouston tenant Tou
3. James Inkster tenant Lerquoy
4. George Inkster tenant Deith
5. John Mouat tenant Breckan
6. William Inksetter tenant Stennesgorn
7. William Hercus tenant Lingrow
8. Alexander Marwick tenant Lewishouse
9. James Flaws tenant Hammersfield
10. William Louttit tenant Netter Breckan
11. Hugh Craigie tenant Seaterquoy
12. Isobel Craigie tenant Ploverhall
13. Barbara Craigie tenant Slackback
14. Peter Lennard tenant Kirkgate
15. John Craigie tenant Galieshaws
16. Elizabeth Craigie tenant Mid Lingrow
17. George Marwick tenant Tealquoy
18. William Gibson tenant Quoys
19. James Peason tenant Houlterburn
20. George Downie tenant Blackhammer
21. Christian Mouat tenant Upper Blackhammer
22. Isobel Inksetter tenant in Grain

On his death on 30th March 1847 , an inventory [56] of George McBeath's shop and household goods was as follows:

Shop goods and furniture total £25 2/- 11 ½ d
Household Furniture:

- Dining Room £54 9/- 5 ½ d
- Parlour £21 1/- 6d
- Small room off parlour £6 17/-
- Bedroom off dining room £5 18/-
- Second bedroom £4 13/- 3d
- Front bedroom £8 17/- 6d
- Back high bedroom £5 7/- 6d
- Small closet bedroom £1 1/-
- Kitchen £5 7/- 4d (includes servants bedding 10/- 6d)
- Wash House £2 18/- 6d
- Store £9 15 /- (includes 5lbs tea = £1 10/-)
- Cart shed £30 4/- 3d
- **TOTAL = £166 10/- 3 ½ d**

George McBeath is buried in St Magnus Cathedral kirkyard. His gravestone reads:

"In memory of GEORGE MCBEATH who died 30th March 1847 aged 47 years. Also of his children ANN who died 23rd October 1840 aged 8 years, MARY ANN who died 26th April 1841 aged 11 days, SAMUEL who died 11th June 1844 aged 7 months, WILLIAM who died 26th September 1844 aged 14 years, JOHN who died 13th June 1866 aged 27 years. Also ISABELLA MAINLAND MCBEATH his widow who died 5th November 1893 aged 91 years. [Flat stone in front – Illegible] St Magnus Cathedral Graveyard, Kirkwall: H/6/31."

George McBeath was only 47 years of age when he died but he had built up a very strong business which his son, James built upon.

James Mainland McBeath (1829 – 1902) also started out in the strawplaiting industry continuing the trade as his father had done. When the industry died James switched to having an ironmongery shop at 10 Albert Street, now occupied by Ortak. He was also involved in shipping.

Other Kirkwall Strawplait Merchants included: Balfour Mainland, John Taylor, and Robert Borwick.

Balfour Mainland became a successful merchant and owner of several properties. In his later years he became blind. He died at Broad Street Kirkwall on the 31st March 1864 aged 76 years.

Correspondence between Kirkwall merchant John Taylor gives an indication of the wheeling and dealing that was going on in the early years of the strawplaiting boom:

1814 – 15th June Letter from Mr Robert Scott, London to John Taylor

Received a box of plait on the 9th.

"I cannot flatter you much on the quality of your platts – the coarse is not worth making up, therefore I was obliged to bring down the price of the best that the worst might go with it. I called at several places with it. Some would make me no offer at all and others would not offer me near your money. So at last I took the liberty of calling on William Pimlett about your other box.

He said that your platt was so bad that he would not have it at any money.

I asked him if he could have the goodness to look at a Box that I had from you which he did. He said it was a great deal better than the Box you sent him.

This is just the height of the business and consequently everyone is overstretched with goods. I sold your Box of platt to Mr Pimlett on the following terms total £27 19/- 6d

Minus expenses – 10/- 7d"

Letter from John Parry, March 10th 1813, 71 Banner Street, Finsbury, London

Complaining about his foreman, Richard Pimlett

"Sincerely sir, had you considered it for one moment you would have seen the impropriety of such conduct on my foreman's part – and acquainted me with his secret intentions, which would have ensured to yourself an agreement with the principal."

He then went on to comment about Pimlett 'taking him in' as to his business ability, suggesting it was an error of judgement to let him in etc.

"He went into my splitting room through the good graces of Mrs Parry – but fortunately in that room I had no other machines than what are commonly made and used in Kirkwall." [57]

Robert Borwick was born in approximately 1768 and died in 1840 aged 72. He introduced strawplaiting to Birsay in 1807 but, because this was so early on in the industry, the records are few. He married Jean Loutit in 1798 and is buried in St Magnus Cathedral kirkyard, Kirkwall.

The gravestone reads:

"[Flat stone] The grave of ROBERT BORWICK, Merchant, Kirkwall, who died 1840 aged 72 years and of JEAN LOUTIT his wife who died 1824 aged 47. Also of their children MARGARET MEUDELL BORWICK who died 1808 in infancy and MARGARET STEWART BORWICK who died 1859 aged 43 years. Also GEORGE BORWICK their oldest son who died 8th Sept 1869 aged 68 years, WILLIAM BORWICK their second son, Purser in the Peninsular and Oriental Steam Companies service, who died at Calcutta 4th Sept 1852 aged 43. He was interred in the Howrah cemetery there and JAMES BORWICK who died 11th July 1892 aged 89 years."

Many other men were also involved in the industry due to the power of Orkney's shipping connections. Men like Oliver Scott who was a friend of Robert Borwick. Oliver Scott became a Magistrate in the town. His gravestone in St Magnus Cathedral kirkyard gives little indication of his previous involvement in the straw plait trade:

"The grave of OLIVER SCOTT, late Merchant in Kirkwall, who died 11th March 1846 aged 88 years. Also of his spouse ANN SPENCE who died 10th February 1831 aged 81 years."

The Stromness Merchants

At the turn of the 19th Century Stromness was a bulging and highly successful port. Basically it was one street running south to north with crowded houses filled with traders, workers, seafarers, shops and strawplaiters.

The Old Statistical Account records that in 1754 the population of the town was 1,000. By 1794 the town and the parish had grown:

	Houses	Families	Males	Females	Total
Stromness parish:	184	184	346	449	795
Stromness town:	222	342	493	851	1344
Total:	406	526	839	1300	2199

Many able bodied men had to leave Orkney for employment: military service, as seafarers, Hudson Bay Company workers, whaling and emigrating. This left thousands of women in the islands as the main provider for the family while the men were away.

Population of Stromness 1841 and 1851 census

Population of Stromness		Males	Females	% Total Strawplaiting	% Females Strawplaiting
1841:	2784	1,094 39%	1,690 61%	11.4%	19%
1851:	2753	1,081 39%	1,672 61%	4.6%	7.6%

Stromness, along with Kirkwall, was where the strawplait and bonnets were shipped from to ports south, travelling as far as traders in London. There were thousands of women employed in the industry in Stromness itself and as a major port, boxes of plait and bonnets were also brought into the town where there were several merchants trading in this commodity.

One of the most successful in Orkney was William Heddle. Born in 1791, Heddle was there at the start of the strawplait boom and as a young man made the most of this opportunity. In 1809 he married Euphemia Leask and together they would have a large family.

William Heddle made a good deal of money from trading in strawplait and he was able to move from Main Street, Stromness, to Quildon, a property of several acres overlooking the town. Like most successful traders he purchased land and holdings and pursued debtors in the courts who owed him money. William Heddle died in 1849 of a 'lingering illness', as the strawplait industry was starting to slow down. There is a large tomb stone erected to him by his wife and children in the Stromness kirkyard.

"Sacred to the mem of WILLIAM HEDDLE Esq of Quildon d 14 May 1849 aged 61, after a lingering illness endured with much Christian resignation & fortitude. Erected by his widow and children."

Andrew Young, born 1790, was another of the Stromness traders in strawplait who was there right at the start of the boom. Young lived in Main Street in the part now known as Alfred Street. As the industry began to wane Andrew Young returned to his work as a pilot. This occupation was a vital part of the busy commercial business of Stromness. His son, Hans was a tailor and daughters Ann and Margaret were seamstresses. This type of work, fine needle skills, were all linked to the strawplait industry. After his death aged 75 in 1855, Andrew Young's wife, Barbara, made a living as a knitter and his children ran a shop with the family living above it.

James Sutherland, born 1801, did not have so many successful years in strawplait trading, but it was sufficient to set him and his wife Cecilia up in a grocer's shop. James outlived his wife and in his 70s was residing with a brother in Dundas Street.

Hugh Leask was in at the very start of the trade but was already elderly and so did not live to see how massive the industry became.

Other Stromness strawplait traders included: James Corrigall, James Louttit, John Flett, John Fraser, John Leask, John Rendall, and Robert Clouston. In a bustling and close knit town as Stromness was, all of these traders would know each other, some would be friendly acquaintances, others not so , for it was a very competitive business.

John Rendall was involved in the industry till its demise when he ran a lodging house and a draper's shop in Church Road. The example of strawplait on display in Stromness Museum which won an award at the 1851 Crystal Palace Great Exhibition is by his wife, Jean.

John Rendall and his wife are buried in Stromness kirkyard. The gravestone is broken but reads:

"In memory of JOHN RENDALL. Merchant, d. 14 Feb 1879 aged 77. JEAN ALLAN, his wife."

The merchants were connected up with the supply and distribution chain, trading the goods onwards. Tied in with shipping and interconnected as these men were with social, family and church ties (especially in the case of the Kirkwall merchants) it is extremely unlikely that a woman, for example, Catherine Tait of Queen Street, Stromness, would be a trader. This is most likely just the way her occupation was recorded by the census taker.

Although it is unlikely that women in Orkney were strawplait merchants that was not the case in England. In her PhD Thesis Catherine Robinson says:

"The impact of such ubiquitous and culturally stable cottage industries during the first half of the 19th century meant that women became very knowledgeable about the straw hat trade.

It appears that following Luton's rapid industrial expansion, women continued to play a significant role in the management of straw hat manufacture, in the many small Luton hat making workshops."[58]

There were many women employed plaiting straw in Queen Street, Stromness and it can be reasonable to assume Catherine Tait would be one of those. Like so many women who had been earning a living as a strawplaiter, once the industry collapsed she earned an income by knitting.

Like all industries which boom and then bust – there are winners and losers. Some of the traders were to make their fortunes enabling them to buy up land and properties. For others the loss of such a lucrative industry meant that they had to find another income source, some would turn to the sea and the work of the port, others to setting up shops or lodging houses, catering for the growing Stromness population.

The end of the straw plait industry in Orkney

By the 1860s the straw plait industry had vanished from the economy of the islands. It was, however, flourishing elsewhere. "By 1870, there were thousands of English plaiters, men as well as women, young and old, who plaited primarily to contribute to their own family economies. The result was a cottage economy environment which produced plaits of varying quality and varying price." [59]

The strawplait industry and that of straw bonnet making had become centralised in the Luton/Dunstable area. The further away from Luton producers were the less they were paid and the higher their transport costs. There was also a fall in the price of plait as Free Trade resulted in imported plait becoming cheaper. This meant that for Orkney the industry was no longer profitable. Shipping and carriage costs alongwith being further away from the buyers produced insurmountable problems. The men who had been in at the beginning of the trade were either now elderly or dead. Younger merchants could try their luck at other trades including employing women once employed as straw plaiters to produce knitted stockings and clothing.

In 1873 Britain went into an economic depression which lasted for years. Plait had been imported from China since the 1860s. The Canton plait, as it was known, was made by workers for a pittance of a wage. It was much cheaper but it wasn't until the depression years that the straw hat manufacturers realised its potential to reach into a new market. Straw hats could now be made at a price affordable by the masses. Luton came to dominate the sector.

In the 1890s the straw plait was imported from Japan and this was at an even cheaper price than that from China. Sewing machines had been introduced into the making of bonnets which had all been stitched by hand. The longer hanks of the cheaper imported strawplait at 60 yards in length was suited to the new machines.

Strawplaiting in Orkney was not some cosy romantic easy going way of earning a living. For the women it employed it was a choice forced upon them by the necessity of earning an income. At its height it was on a massive scale with even the very young being employed. Mechanisation, centralised and based in large manufacturing workshops, brought about the end of what had been a profitable industry in Orkney for over 50 years. It was replaced by knitting which was to continue as a source of income for island women till well into the 20th Century.

This period was a time of great change in Orkney. A time when landlordism changed the landscape and removed tenants from their farms. There was a continual drift of population from the rural areas and into the towns of Stromness and Kirkwall. Able bodied young men had to leave the islands to find work at sea or with employers like the Hudson Bay Company.

"It was not always of their own choice that men left the land for other jobs. Because Britain was at war with France men were required for the navy. Hundreds of Orkneymen served in Nelson's ships…A proportion of these men may have volunteered to serve, but others had been caught and forced to enlist by the Press Gang."[60]

Women outnumbered the men across the parishes and had to provide for their families whatever way they could. With so many young men serving years away abroad, for the young women who were left running the farms, strawplaiting and knitting - marriage passed them by. They were to remain single to the end of their days often living with sisters or other family members.

This short publication looking at the strawplaiting industry in Orkney and the people, mostly women, who worked in it, will hopefully be of use to future researchers to delve more into this fascinating but overlooked manufacture in the islands' history.

80

Notes & References

1. Quote from Martin Chuzzlewitt, by Charles Dickens, chapter 22. (1842)
2. Aura Tortosa, J. & Pérez-Jordà, Guillem & Carrión, Yolanda & Seguí, Joan & Jordá Pardo, Jesús & Miret Estruch, Carles & Verdasco, Carlos. (2020). Cordage, basketry and containers at the Pleistocene–Holocene boundary in southwest Europe. Evidence from Coves de Santa Maira (Valencian region, Spain). Vegetation History and Archaeobotany. 29. 581-594. 10.1007/s00334-019-00758-x.
3. Luton: Hat Industry 1750 to 2000, A Local History Resource Pack Luton Museum Education Service
4. Pamela Horn The Buckinghamshire Straw Plait Trade in Victorian England
5. Luton: Hat Industry 1750 to 2000, A Local History Resource Pack Luton Museum Education Service
6. Nigel Goose, Population Economy and Family Structure in Hertfordshire in 1851. Vol. 1. The Berkhamsted Region (Hatfield, 1996), p.44
7. Pamela Horn The Buckinghamshire Straw Plait Trade in Victorian England
8. Orkney Herald and Advertiser, 7th November 1894, 'Manufacture of Straw Articles in Orkney' by Walter T. Dension for Orkney Natural History Society
9. ch 12 'A Straw in the wind Making history with a bonnet' by Fiona McKergow in History Making a Difference, New Approaches from Aotearoa, ed Katie Pickles, Lyndon Fraser, Marguerite Hill, Sarah Murray and Greg Ryan, Cambridge Scholars Publishing 2017
10. The New History of Orkney, William P.L. Thomson, published by Mercat Press
11. Statistical Account of Orkney Parish of Sandwick, The Rev Charles Clouston, Minister

12. Statistical Account of Orkney, Parish of Kirkwall and St Ola, The Rev William Logie, Minister
13. The Dundee Advertiser 17th August 1898
14. 'Straw Plaiting', https://www.rectorylanecemetery.org.uk/articles/straw-plaiting/
15. The New History of Orkney, William P.L. Thomson, published by Mercat Press
16. Statistical Account of Orkney United Parishes of Birsay and Harray, The Rev Thomas Blyth, Minister
17. Statistical Account of Orkney United Parishes of Birsay and Harray, The Rev Thomas Blyth, Minister
18. Statistical Account of Orkney, Parish of Kirkwall and St Ola, The Rev William Logie, Minister
19. Statistical Account of Orkney, Parish of Kirkwall and St Ola, The Rev William Logie, Minister
20. Statistical Account of Orkney United Parishes of Birsay and Harray, The Rev Thomas Blyth, Minister
21. Statistical Account of Orkney United Parishes of Birsay and Harray, The Rev Thomas Blyth, Minister
22. Statistical Account of Orkney United Parishes of Birsay and Harray, The Rev Thomas Blyth, Minister
23. Statistical Account of Orkney Parish of St Andrews and Deerness, Rev James Smellie, Minister
24. The Fame of Hull https://en.wikipedia.org/wiki/Fame_(1786_ship)
25. Statistical Account of Orkney, United Parishes of Eday and Pharay Rev John Simpson, Minister
26. Statistical Account of Orkney, United Parishes of Eday and Pharay Rev John Simpson, Minister
27. Statistical Account of Orkney, United Parishes of Evie and Rendall, The Rev David Pitcairn
28. Statistical Account of Orkney, United Parishes of Evie and Rendall, The Rev David Pitcairn
29. Statistical Account of Orkney, United Parishes of Evie and Rendall, The Rev David Pitcairn
30. Orkney Herald and Advertiser, 27th of December 1916

31. Statistical Account of Orkney, Parish of Firth and Stenness, Rev William Malcolm, Minister
32. Statistical Account of Orkney United Parishes of Birsay and Harray Rev Thomas Blyth, Minister
33. Statistical Account of Orkney United Parishes of Birsay and Harray, Rev Thomas Blyth, Minister
34. Statistical Account of Orkney, United Parish of Holme and Paplay, The Rev Andrew Smith Minister
35. Statistical Account of Orkney, Parish of Kirkwall and St Ola, The Rev William Logie, Minister
36. Statistical Account of Orkney, Parish of Kirkwall and St Ola, The Rev William Logie, Minister
37. Statistical Account of Orkney, Parish of Kirkwall and St Ola, The Rev William Logie, Minister
38. Statistical Account of Orkney, Parish of Kirkwall and St Ola, The Rev William Logie, Minister
39. Statistical Account of Orkney, Parish of Kirkwall and St Ola, The Rev William Logie, Minister
40. Statistical Account of Orkney, Parish of Kirkwall and St Ola, The Rev William Logie, Minister
41. Death of Janet Flett, [OPR Death: 1853-021-00-70-p264-10], accessed via Orkney Family History Society, https://orkneyfhs.co.uk
42. Statistical Account of Orkney, Parish of Sandwick, The Rev Charles Clouston, Minister
43. Statistical Account of Orkney, Parish of Stromness, The Rev Peter Learmonth, Minister
44. Statistical Account of Orkney, United Parishes of Stronsay and Eday, The Rev John Simpson, Minister
45. Statistical Account of Orkney, United Parishes of Walls and Flotta, The Rev Walter Weir, Minister
46. Statistical Account of Orkney, Parish of Westray, The Rev John Armit, Minister
47. Orkney Herald 25 December 1866
48. Three generations of Batchelors – the rise and fall of a straw plaiting family www.chilternsaonb.org/news

49. Ref Orkney Archives D9/6 Taylor Papers. Letter from David
    Ramsay to John Taylor (merchant Kirkwall) 20th July 1813
50. The Dundee Advertiser 17th August 1898
51. The Dundee Advertiser 17th August 1898
52. Orkney Archives SC11/38/4 p 465 28th February 1854
    Inventory of David Ramsay d. 2nd August 1853
53. Orkney Herald – 6th Feb 1895
54. Orkney Archives SC11/5/1839/078 Sheriff Court Records –
    Civil Court Processes 1839
55. Orkney Archives SC11/5/1838/037 Sheriff Court Records –
    Civil Court Processes 1838
56. Orkney Archives SC11/38/3 Orkney Sheriff Court Register of
    Inventories 1st February 1848
57. Orkney Archives D 9/6 Taylor Papers – John Taylor Merchant of
    Kirkwall
58. Catherine Robinson, p 62 "Imports, Mechanisation and the
    Decline of the English Plaiting Industry: the View from the
    Hatters' Gazette, Luton 1873-1900"
59. Catherine Robinson, p 62 "Imports, Mechanisation and the
    Decline of the English Plaiting Industry: the View from the
    Hatters' Gazette, Luton 1873-1900"
60. An Orkney Anthology, Selected Works Ernest Walker Marwick,
    by John D.M.Robertson published by Scottish Academic Press

Comparison of data 1841 and 1851 Orkney strawplaiters

	1841	1851
Birsay	128	164
Deerness	28	19
Eday Faray	12	1
Evie Rendall Gairsay	16	43
Firth Stenness	23	28
Harray	133	48
Holm Paplay	0	6
Hoy Graemsay	16	5
Kirkwall St Ola	334	149
North Ronaldsay	0	0
Orphir	68	22
Rousay Egilsay Wyre	28	15
St Andrews	27	15
Sanday	14	9
Sandwick	93	58
Shapinsay	32	7
South Ronaldsay Burray	77	4
Stromness	317	127
Stronsay	17	10
Walls Flotta	1	0
Westray Papa Westray	8	0
Total	**1,372**	**730**

Population graphs of Strawplaiters

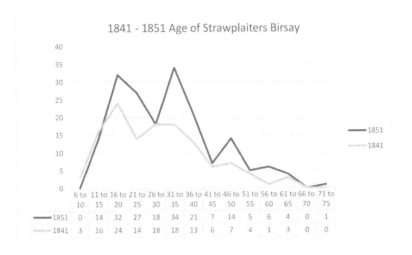

1841 - 1851 Age of Strawplaiters Birsay

	6 to 10	11 to 15	16 to 20	21 to 25	26 to 30	31 to 35	36 to 40	41 to 45	46 to 50	51 to 55	56 to 60	61 to 65	66 to 70	71 to 75
1851	0	14	32	27	18	34	21	7	14	5	6	4	0	1
1841	3	16	24	14	18	18	13	6	7	4	1	3	0	0

Marital Status of Strawplaiters Birsay 1851

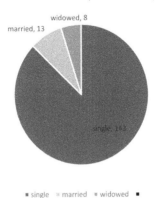

widowed, 8
married, 13
single, 143

■ single ■ married ■ widowed ■

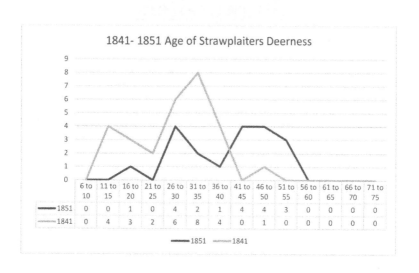

1841- 1851 Age of Strawplaiters Deerness

	6 to 10	11 to 15	16 to 20	21 to 25	26 to 30	31 to 35	36 to 40	41 to 45	46 to 50	51 to 55	56 to 60	61 to 65	66 to 70	71 to 75
1851	0	0	1	0	4	2	1	4	4	3	0	0	0	0
1841	0	4	3	2	6	8	4	0	1	0	0	0	0	0

1851   1841

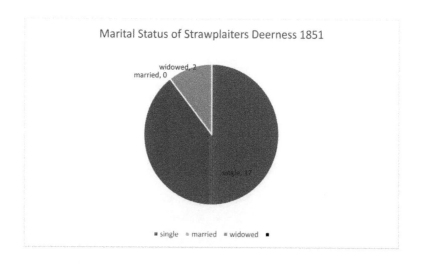

Marital Status of Strawplaiters Deerness 1851

widowed, 2
married, 0

single, 17

■ single   ■ married   ■ widowed   ■

88

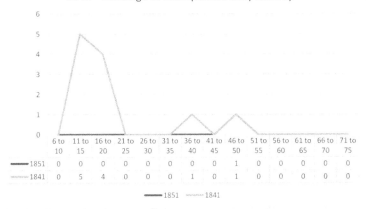

1841 - 1851 Age of Strawplaiters Eday & Faray

	6 to 10	11 to 15	16 to 20	21 to 25	26 to 30	31 to 35	36 to 40	41 to 45	46 to 50	51 to 55	56 to 60	61 to 65	66 to 70	71 to 75
1851	0	0	0	0	0	0	0	0	1	0	0	0	0	0
1841	0	5	4	0	0	0	1	0	1	0	0	0	0	0

———1851 ········1841

Marital Status of Strawplaiters Eday and Faray 1851

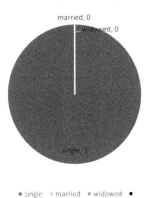

married, 0
widowed, 0

single, 1

■ single ■ married ■ widowed ■

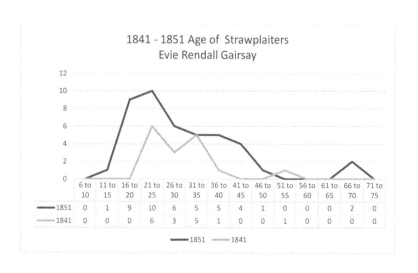

1841 - 1851 Age of Strawplaiters
Evie Rendall Gairsay

	6 to 10	11 to 15	16 to 20	21 to 25	26 to 30	31 to 35	36 to 40	41 to 45	46 to 50	51 to 55	56 to 60	61 to 65	66 to 70	71 to 75
1851	0	1	9	10	6	5	5	4	1	0	0	0	2	0
1841	0	0	0	6	3	5	1	0	0	1	0	0	0	0

1851 1841

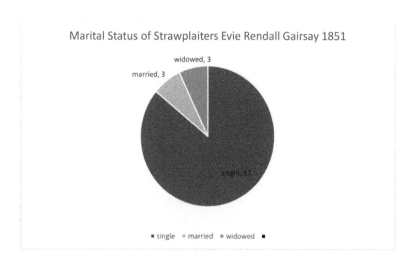

Marital Status of Strawplaiters Evie Rendall Gairsay 1851

widowed, 3

married, 3

single, 37

single   married   widowed

90

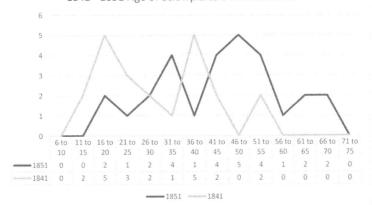

1841 - 1851 Age of Strawplaiters Firth Stenness

	6 to 10	11 to 15	16 to 20	21 to 25	26 to 30	31 to 35	36 to 40	41 to 45	46 to 50	51 to 55	56 to 60	61 to 65	66 to 70	71 to 75
1851	0	0	2	1	2	4	1	4	5	4	1	2	2	0
1841	0	2	5	3	2	1	5	2	0	2	0	0	0	0

— 1851 — 1841

Marital Status of Strawplaiters Firth Stenness 1851

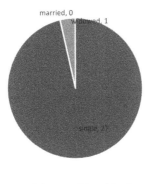

married, 0

widowed, 1

single, 27

■ single ■ married ■ widowed

91

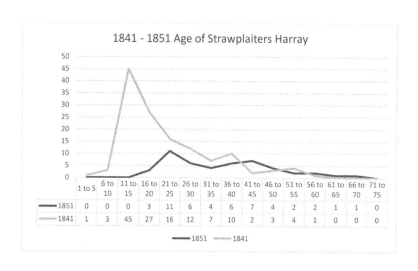

1841 - 1851 Age of Strawplaiters Harray

	1 to 5	6 to 10	11 to 15	16 to 20	21 to 25	26 to 30	31 to 35	36 to 40	41 to 45	46 to 50	51 to 55	56 to 60	61 to 65	66 to 70	71 to 75
1851	0	0	0	3	11	6	4	6	7	4	2	2	1	1	0
1841	1	3	45	27	16	12	7	10	2	3	4	1	0	0	0

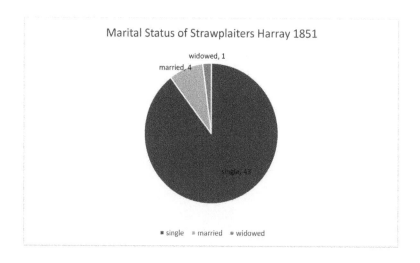

Marital Status of Strawplaiters Harray 1851

widowed, 1
married, 4
single, 43

■ single ■ married ■ widowed

1851 Age of Strawplaiters Holm and Paplay

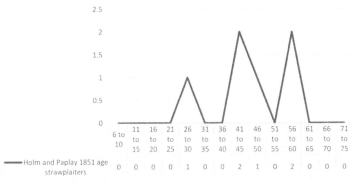

	6 to 10	11 to 15	16 to 20	21 to 25	26 to 30	31 to 35	36 to 40	41 to 45	46 to 50	51 to 55	56 to 60	61 to 65	66 to 70	71 to 75
Holm and Paplay 1851 age strawplaiters	0	0	0	0	1	0	0	2	1	0	2	0	0	0

Holm and Paplay 1851 age strawplaiters

Marital Status of Strawplaiters Holm Paplay 1851

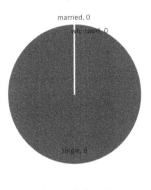

married, 0
widowed, 0
single, 6

• single • married • widowed

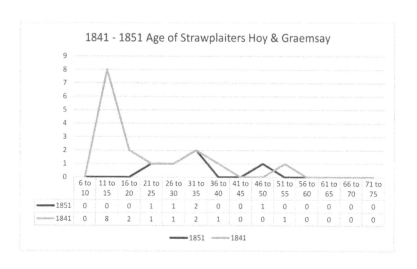

1841 - 1851 Age of Strawplaiters Hoy & Graemsay

	6 to 10	11 to 15	16 to 20	21 to 25	26 to 30	31 to 35	36 to 40	41 to 45	46 to 50	51 to 55	56 to 60	61 to 65	66 to 70	71 to 75
1851	0	0	0	1	1	2	0	0	1	0	0	0	0	0
1841	0	8	2	1	1	2	1	0	0	1	0	0	0	0

1851 ——— 1841

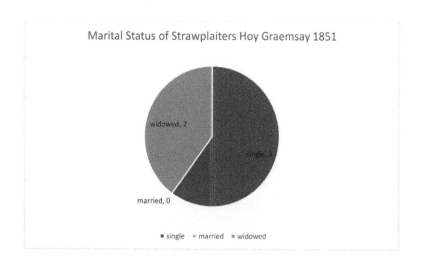

Marital Status of Strawplaiters Hoy Graemsay 1851

widowed, 2

single, 3

married, 0

■ single ■ married ■ widowed

94

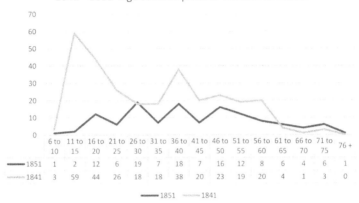

1841 - 1851 Age of Strawplaiters Kirkwall & St Ola

	6 to 10	11 to 15	16 to 20	21 to 25	26 to 30	31 to 35	36 to 40	41 to 45	46 to 50	51 to 55	56 to 60	61 to 65	66 to 70	71 to 75	76 +
1851	1	2	12	6	19	7	18	7	16	12	8	6	4	6	1
1841	3	59	44	26	18	18	38	20	23	19	20	4	1	3	0

1851   1841

Marital Status of Strawplaiters Kirkwall St Ola 1851

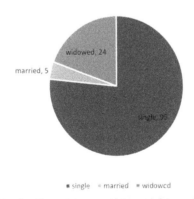

widowed, 24

married, 5

single, 95

single   married   widowed

95

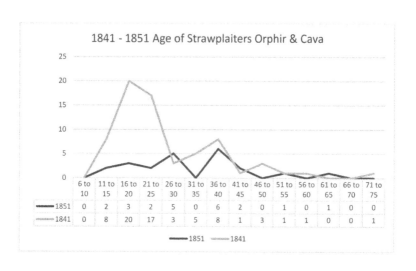

	6 to 10	11 to 15	16 to 20	21 to 25	26 to 30	31 to 35	36 to 40	41 to 45	46 to 50	51 to 55	56 to 60	61 to 65	66 to 70	71 to 75
1851	0	2	3	2	5	0	6	2	0	1	0	1	0	0
1841	0	8	20	17	3	5	8	1	3	1	1	0	0	1

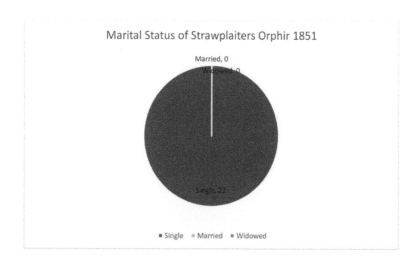

1841 - 1851 Age of Strawplaiters Rousay Egilsay Wyre

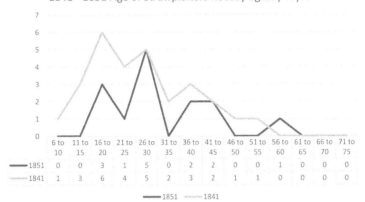

	6 to 10	11 to 15	16 to 20	21 to 25	26 to 30	31 to 35	36 to 40	41 to 45	46 to 50	51 to 55	56 to 60	61 to 65	66 to 70	71 to 75
1851	0	0	3	1	5	0	2	2	0	0	1	0	0	0
1841	1	3	6	4	5	2	3	2	1	1	0	0	0	0

━━━ 1851   ┈┈┈ 1841

Marital Status of Strawplaiters Rousay Egilsay Wyre 1851

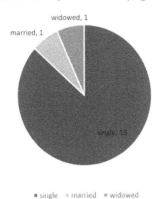

widowed, 1

married, 1

single, 13

■ single   ■ married   ■ widowed

97

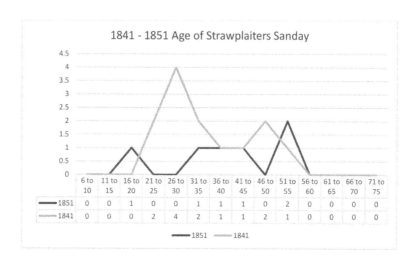

1841 - 1851 Age of Strawplaiters Sanday

	6 to 10	11 to 15	16 to 20	21 to 25	26 to 30	31 to 35	36 to 40	41 to 45	46 to 50	51 to 55	56 to 60	61 to 65	66 to 70	71 to 75
1851	0	0	1	0	0	1	1	1	0	2	0	0	0	0
1841	0	0	0	2	4	2	1	1	2	1	0	0	0	0

1851   1841

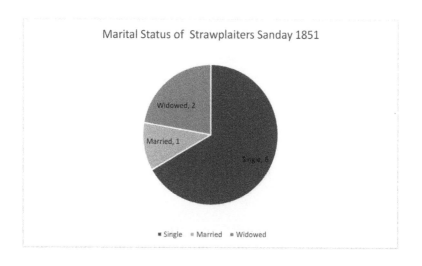

Marital Status of Strawplaiters Sanday 1851

Widowed, 2

Married, 1

Single, 8

■ Single   ■ Married   ■ Widowed

98

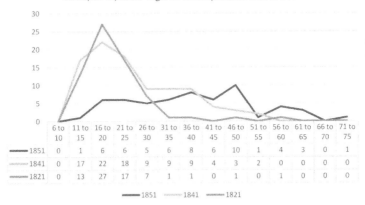

1821,1841,1851 Age of Strawplaiters Sandwick

	6 to 10	11 to 15	16 to 20	21 to 25	26 to 30	31 to 35	36 to 40	41 to 45	46 to 50	51 to 55	56 to 60	61 to 65	66 to 70	71 to 75
1851	0	1	6	6	5	6	8	6	10	1	4	3	0	1
1841	0	17	22	18	9	9	9	4	3	2	0	0	0	0
1821	0	13	27	17	7	1	1	0	1	0	1	0	0	0

1851   1841   1821

Marital Status of Strawplaiters Sandwick 1851

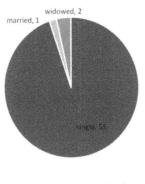

widowed, 2
married, 1

single, 55

■ single   ■ married   ■ widowed

99

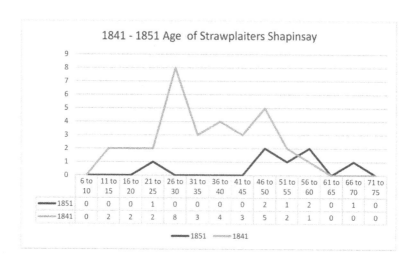

1841 - 1851 Age of Strawplaiters Shapinsay

	6 to 10	11 to 15	16 to 20	21 to 25	26 to 30	31 to 35	36 to 40	41 to 45	46 to 50	51 to 55	56 to 60	61 to 65	66 to 70	71 to 75
1851	0	0	0	1	0	0	0	0	2	1	2	0	1	0
1841	0	2	2	2	8	3	4	3	5	2	1	0	0	0

1851   1841

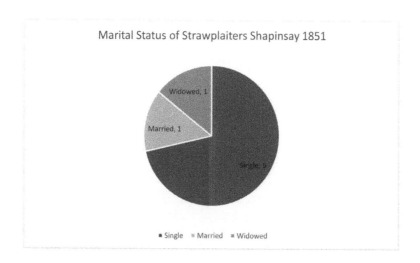

Marital Status of Strawplaiters Shapinsay 1851

Widowed, 1

Married, 1

Single, 5

■ Single   ■ Married   ■ Widowed

100

1841 - 1851 Age of Strawplaiters South Ronaldsay & Burray

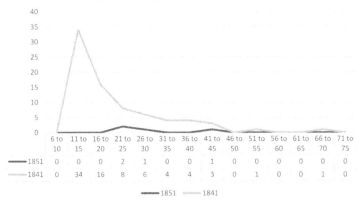

	6 to 10	11 to 15	16 to 20	21 to 25	26 to 30	31 to 35	36 to 40	41 to 45	46 to 50	51 to 55	56 to 60	61 to 65	66 to 70	71 to 75
1851	0	0	0	2	1	0	0	1	0	0	0	0	0	0
1841	0	34	16	8	6	4	4	3	0	1	0	0	1	0

━━━1851 ⋯⋯⋯ 1841

Marital Status of Strawplaiters South Ronaldsay Burray 1851

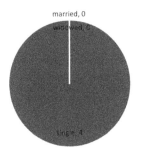

■ single ■ married ■ widowed

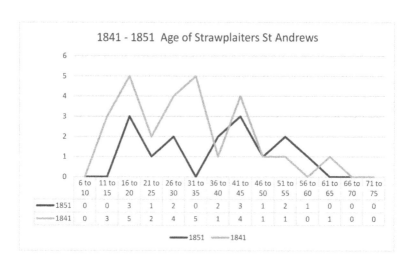

	6 to 10	11 to 15	16 to 20	21 to 25	26 to 30	31 to 35	36 to 40	41 to 45	46 to 50	51 to 55	56 to 60	61 to 65	66 to 70	71 to 75
1851	0	0	3	1	2	0	2	3	1	2	1	0	0	0
1841	0	3	5	2	4	5	1	4	1	1	0	1	0	0

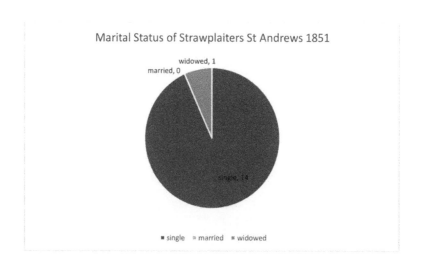

1821, 1841, 1851 Age of Strawplaiters Stromness

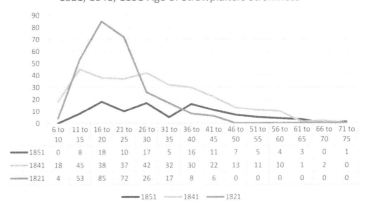

	6 to 10	11 to 15	16 to 20	21 to 25	26 to 30	31 to 35	36 to 40	41 to 45	46 to 50	51 to 55	56 to 60	61 to 65	66 to 70	71 to 75
1851	0	8	18	10	17	5	16	11	7	5	4	3	0	1
1841	18	45	38	37	42	32	30	22	13	11	10	1	2	0
1821	4	53	85	72	26	17	8	6	0	0	0	0	0	0

━━ 1851 ━━ 1841 ━━ 1821

Marital Status of Strawplaiters Stromness 1851

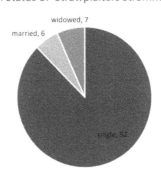

■ single ■ married ■ widowed

103

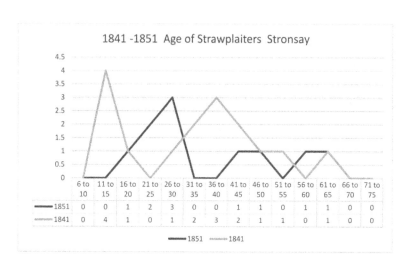

1841 -1851 Age of Strawplaiters Stronsay

	6 to 10	11 to 15	16 to 20	21 to 25	26 to 30	31 to 35	36 to 40	41 to 45	46 to 50	51 to 55	56 to 60	61 to 65	66 to 70	71 to 75
1851	0	0	1	2	3	0	0	1	1	0	1	1	0	0
1841	0	4	1	0	1	2	3	2	1	1	0	1	0	0

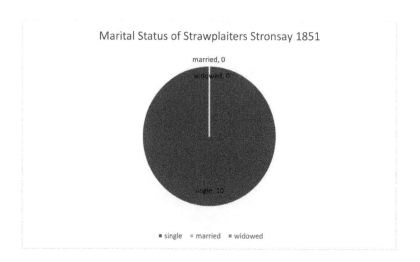

Marital Status of Strawplaiters Stronsay 1851

married, 0

widowed, 0

single, 10

■ single ■ married ■ widowed

1841 -1851 Age of Strawplaiters Walls and Flotta

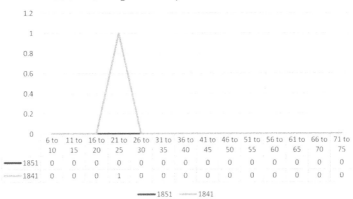

	6 to 10	11 to 15	16 to 20	21 to 25	26 to 30	31 to 35	36 to 40	41 to 45	46 to 50	51 to 55	56 to 60	61 to 65	66 to 70	71 to 75
1851	0	0	0	0	0	0	0	0	0	0	0	0	0	0
1841	0	0	0	1	0	0	0	0	0	0	0	0	0	0

1851 ——— 1841

1841 -1851 Age of Strawplaiters Westray Papa Westray

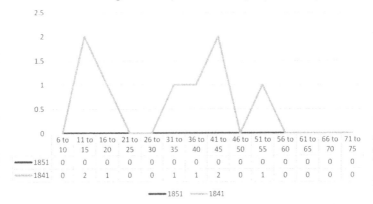

	6 to 10	11 to 15	16 to 20	21 to 25	26 to 30	31 to 35	36 to 40	41 to 45	46 to 50	51 to 55	56 to 60	61 to 65	66 to 70	71 to 75
1851	0	0	0	0	0	0	0	0	0	0	0	0	0	0
1841	0	2	1	0	0	1	1	2	0	1	0	0	0	0

1851 ——— 1841

1821 Census Records of Strawplaiters

Name	Address	Age	Notes
Helen Sabiston	Lower Quoy, Quoy, Sandwick	24	
Jannet Tours	Vinbrek Voy Sandwick	15	
Margaret Moar	Trot(a cot house)Voy Sandwick	19	
Catherine Kirkness	Upper Lyking Sandwick	15	
Elizabeth Harvey	Skithva Sandwick	14	
Isabella Harvey	Skithva Sandwick	12	
Christine Brown	Ness Wasbister Sandwick	21	
Margaret Brown	Ness Wasbister Sandwick	18	
Betty Brown	Ness Wasbister Sandwick	16	
Jean Marwick	Appiton Wasbister Sandwick	24	
Mary Marwick	Appiton Wasbister Sandwick	22	
Isabella Marwick	Appiton Wasbister Sandwick	15	
Isabella Spence	Appiton Wasbister Sandwick	14	
Betty Brown	Appihouse Wasbister Sandwick	22	
Jannet Brown	Appihouse Wasbister Sandwick	20	
Jannet Johnston	East House Tenston Sandwick	27	
Jannet Louttit	Quoys Tenston Sandwick	24	
Mary Louttit	Quoys Tenston Sandwick	23	
Betty Louttit	Quoys Tenston Sandwick	16	
Margaret Sabeston	Fawell Tenston Sandwick	27	
Jannet Sabeston	Fawell Tenston Sandwick	17	
Elizabeth Stockine	Breck Cott Tenston Sandwick	27	
Elizabeth Bews	Scaraton Tenston Sandwick	14	
Christy Garson	Vetquoy Tenston Sandwick	20	
Elspet Garson	Vetquoy Tenston Sandwick	18	
Catherine Garson	Vetquoy Tenston Sandwick	13	
Sibella Smith	Downby Hourston Sandwick	26	
Elspeth Smith	Downby Hourston Sandwick	24	
Christian Hourston	Upperhouse Hourston Sandwick	17	
Catherine Hourston	East House Hourston Sandwick	19	
Ann Hourston	East House Hourston Sandwick	17	
Jannet Merriman	Wart Sandwick	48	
Margaret Smith	Nether Unigar N. Unigar Sandwick	23	
Jannet Garson	Outbreck N.Unigar Sandwick	13	
Margaret Kirkness	Gilly North Dyke Sandwick	31	
Margaret Garson	Fidge Skebra Sandwick	24	
Margaret Smirh	Swataway Skebra Sandwick	16	
Jannet Twatt	Nether Bigging Skebra Sandwick	20	
Margaret Twatt	Nether Bigging Skebra Sandwick	18	
Catherine Twatt	Nether Bigging Skebra Sandwick	16	

Ann Corrigall	Bua Skebra Sandwick	24
Margaret Corrigall	Bua Skebra Sandwick	22
Catherine Corrigall	Bua Skebra Sandwick	19
Ann Kirkness	Highland Tronston Sandwick	
Elspet Kirkness	Highland Tronston Sandwick	22
Ann Merriman	Perks Housegarth Sandwick	20
Jannet Tours	Mire Housegarth Sandwick	57
Helen Stockine	Mire Housegarth Sandwick	28
Alexander Brass	Quarrybank Housegarth Sandwick	20
Thomas Brass	Quarrybank Housegarth Sandwick	18
James Brass	Quarrybank Housegarth Sandwick	16
Jannet Brass	Quarrybank Housegarth Sandwick	14
Jannet Brown	Qunina Hestwall Sandwick	30
Chris Sleater	Bean Hestwall Sandwick	17
Mary Flett	Fia Hestwall Sandwick	21
Helen Sleater	Trinnigar Aithstown Sandwick	23
Catherine Sleater	Trinnigar Aithstown Sandwick	17
Catherine Rouland	Hammer Aithstown Sandwick	25
Elizabeth Rouland	Hammer Aithstown Sandwick	19
James Irvine	Eath Aithstown Sandwick	19
Catherine Spence	Landay Naigar Sandwick	17
Margaret Peace	Lee Yesnaby Sandwick	26
Elizabeth Peace	Lee Yesnaby Sandwick	20
Ann Peace	Lee Yesnaby Sandwick	12
Margaret Rouland	Nebigar Southerquoy Sandwick	25
Marjorie Marwick	Garigar Southerquoy Sandwick	38
Elizabeth Linklater	Valzie Southerquoy Sandwick	16
Ann Flett	Skaill Southerquoy Sandwick	14
Catherine Sabeson	Clumley Sandwick	13
Janet Corrigall	1/7/7 Stromness	15
Hannah Corrigall	1/7/7 Stromness	17
Isabella Anderson	1/9/8 Stromness	21
Ann Irvine	1/15/12 Stromness	19
Isabella Irvine	1/27/19 Stromness	31
Ann Banks	1/28/20 Stromness	19
Betty Hourston	1/44/30 Stromness	20
Catherine Gray	1/48/33 Stromness	21
Catherine Ballantine	1/49/33 Stromness	16
Jean Angus	1/52/35 Stromness	19
Clementina Miller	1/62/41 Stromness	35
Jean Leask	1/63/41 Stromness	19
Isabella Sinclair	1/64/42 Stromness	19
Jean Irvine	1/65/43 Stromness	17
Eliz Stewart	1/70/47 Stromness	15
Cath Sinclair	1/71/48 Stromness	16
Charlotte Mirriman	1/76/52 Stromness	14
Margaret Wylie	1/84/58 Stromness	19

Name	Reference	Age	Notes
Betty Wylie	1/84/58 Stromness	18	
Ann Wylie	1/84/58 Stromness	15	
Andrew Young	1/90/64 Stromness	41	straw manufacturer
Eliza Muir	1/98/70 Stromness	12	
Jean Rich	1/99/70 Stromness	24	
Isabella Rich	1/99/70 Stromness	22	
Margaret Harper	1/104/72 Stromness	22	
Jannet Harper	1/104/72 Stromness	20	
Margaret Velzian	1/107/74 Stromness	14	
Jean Wards	1/108/75 Stromness	24	
Bella Sabiston	1/109/76 Stromness	15	
May Sabiston	1/109/76 Stromness	13	
Euphemia Moar	1/111/77 Stromness	18	
Jess Taitt	1/112/78 Stromness	17	
Barbara Lyon	1/113/78 Stromness	41	old maid strawplaiting
Margaret Inkster	1/114/79 Stromness	42	
Ann Inkster	1/114/79 Stromness		widow
Jannet Garson	1/120/83 Stromness	35	
Jannet Dinnet	1/112/85 Stromness	18	
Christ Dinnet	1/112/85 Stromness	16	
Isabella Corrigall	1/123/85 Stromness	16	
Cath Robertson	1/127/87 Stromness	16	
Margaret Linklater	1/130/89 Stromness	23	
Cathrine Brown	1/132/91 Stromness	18	
Marjory Rich	1/138 Stromness	19	
Clementina Oman	1/139/96 Stromness	15	
Mary Oman	1/139/96 Stromness	23	
Cathrine Stanger	Knockhall Stromness	20	
Jannet Yorston	Kingshouse Stromness	34	
Christian Moar	1/146/102 Stromness	38	
Jannet Melvine	1/148/103 Stromness	35	
Isabella Taitt	1/151/105 Stromness	30	
Marjory Knarston	1/155/109 Stromness	25	
Cecilia Wood	1/159/111 Stromness	19	
Jean Wood	1/159/111 Stromness	17	
Isabella Sabiston	1/160/112 Stromness	15	
Margaret Brock	1/162/114 Stromness	25	
Jean Gray	1/168/116 Stromness	26	
Catharine Gray	1/168/116 Stromness	15	
Jean White	1/181/121 Stromness	24	
Jannet Harvey	1/182/121 Stromness	25	
Nelly Harvey	1/182/121 Stromness	22	
Isabella Irvine	1/188/126 Stromness	14	
Ann Linklater	1/190/128 Stromness	25	
Sally Linklater	1/190/128 Stromness	16	
John Flett	1/200/134 Stromness	41	straw manufacturer
Ann Louttit	1/201/135 Stromness	27	

Name	Reference	Age	Occupation
May Louttit	1/201/135 Stromness	21	
Christian Gray	1/202/135 Stromness	30	
Jean Skethaway	1/207/137 Stromness	38	
Margaret Inkster	1/207/137 Stromness	45	
Cameron McKay (F)	1/207/137 Stromness	35	
Isabella Hackland	1/208/138 Stromness	20	
Isabella Clouston	1/212/139 Stromness	15	
Margaret Anderson	1/218/143 Stromness	20	
Betty Anderson	1/218/143 Stromness	17	
Isabella Brock	1/220/144 Stromness	17	
Catherine Yorston	1/221/145 Stromness	28	
Mary Brown	1/232/151 Stromness	35	
Margaret White	1/235/154 Stromness	24	
Eliz White	1/235/154 Stromness	20	
Grizel Firth	1/238/157 Stromness	35	
Betty Watts	1/239/158 Stromness	25	
Margaret Watts	1/239/158 Stromness	23	
Mary Watts	1/239/158 Stromness	15	
Margaret Goudie	1/240/159 Stromness	20	
Helen Young	1/242/159 Stromness	29	
Harriot Stevenson	1/244/161 Stromness	18	bonnet maker
Bella Brodie	1/246/162 Stromness	22	
Cath Rendall	1/247/163 Stromness	21	
Margaret Ricch	1/249/163 Stromness	22	
Sally Esson	1/251/164 Stromness	29	
Ann Esson	1/251/164 Stromness	26	
William Heddle	1/256/166 Stromness	31	straw manufacturer
Isabella Spence	1/257/167 Stromness	33	
Cath Spence	1/257/167 Stromness	22	
Ann Borwick	1/259/168 Stromness	32	
Margaret Borwick	1/259/168 Stromness	26	
Helen Borwick	1/259/168 Stromness	18	
Cath Isbister	1/266/174 Stromness	21	
Cath Ellison	1/275/183 Stromness	22	
Ann Hunton	1/278/184 Stromness	29	
Cath Hunto	1/278/184 Stromness	22	
Margaret Sinclair	1/279/185 Stromness	16	
Fanny Sinclair	1/279/185 Stromness	18	
Cath Bell	1/287/193 Stromness	18	
Jannet Bell	1/287/193 Stromness	14	
Ann Taitt	1/294/197 Stromness	15	
Margaret Hackland	1/295/198 Stromness	25	
Jannet Mowat	1/297/199 Stromness	22	
Anne Mowat	1/297/199 Stromness	21	
Ann Robertson	1/298/200 Stromness	22	
Hugh Leask	1/306/208 Stromness	62	straw manufacturer
John Leask	1/307/208 Stromness	68	straw manufacturer

Betsy Leask	1/307/208 Stromness	23	
Christiana Fraser	1/308/209 Stromness	30	
Margaret Brown	1/310/209 Stromness	23	
Margaret Louttit	1/318/214 Stromness	20	
John Fraser	1/321/217 Stromness	36	straw manufacturer
Ann Taylor	1/322/217 Stromness	26	
Betty Clouston	1/322/217 Stromness	22	
Hannah Rowland	1/322/217 Stromness	24	
Helen Stewart	1/323/217 Stromness	36	
James Louttit	1/328/221 Stromness	32	shipmaster/straw manufacturer
Barbara Leask	1/341/231 Stromness	25	
Ann Belly	1/343/231 Stromness	22	
Christian Robertson	1/344/231 Stromness	25	
Ann Wood	1/356/238 Stromness	20	
Margaret Sabeston	1/358/240 Stromness	12	
Janet Robertson	1/359/240 Stromness	21	
Margaret Philips	1/359/240 Stromness	20	
Frances Turner	1/366/245 Stromness	20	
Catherine Johnston	1/375/251 Stromness	25	
Margaret Clouston	1/376/252 Stromness	27	
Robert Clouston	1/377/252 Stromness	36	straw manufacturer
Betty Johnston	1/378/252 Stromness	25	
Margaret Corrigall	1/378/252 Stromness	13	
Margaret Harvey	1/379/253 Stromness	15	
Betty Corrigall	1/380/253 Stromness	23	
Ann Corrigall	1/380/253 Stromness	19	
Margaret Corston	1/381/254 Stromness	25	
John Corston	1/381/254 Stromness	22	
Mary Corston	1/381/254 Stromness	19	
John Clouston	1/382/255 Stromness	53	straw cutter
Ann Beatton	1/384/255 Stromness	26	
Barbara Roberston	1/385/256 Stromness	22	
Margaret Sabiston	1/386/256 Stromness	42	
Catherine Taitt	1/392/259 Stromness	20	
Isabella Allan	1/392/259 Stromness	20	
Margaret Hackland	1/397/263 Stromness	26	
Isabella Hackland	1/397/263 Stromness	22	
Marjory Hackland	1/397/263 Stromness	20	
Margaret Flett	1/398/264 Stromness	20	
Isabella Watt	1/404/266 Stromness	24	
Barbara Robertson	1/406/267 Stromness	18	
Betty Spence	1/409/269 Stromness	19	
Cath Hunto	1/411/271 Stromness	20	
Jean Copland	1/412/272 Stromness	21	
Jannet Copland	1/412/272 Stromness	15	
Betty Leask	1/413/273 Stromness	14	
Margaret Leask	1/413/273 Stromness	11	

111

Jannet Spence	1/416/276	Stromness	27
Christian Smith	1/422/278	Stromness	25
Mary Foster	1/424/280	Stromness	24
Margaret Brass	1/432/287	Stromness	24
Helen Spence	1/434/289	Stromness	24
Jannet Fiddlar	1/436/291	Stromness	21
May Fiddlar	1/436/291	Stromness	17
Bella Garrioch	1/437/292	Stromness	18
Fanny Mowat	1/422/297	Stromness	22
Marjory Mowat	1/422/297	Stromness	21
Cath Mowat	1/422/297	Stromness	20
Eliz Mowat	1/422/297	Stromness	19
Isoble Brodie	1/443/298	Stromness	35
Cath Sinclair	1/446/301	Stromness	17
Wilhemina Sinclair	1/446/301	Stromness	13
Barbara Sinclair	1/446/301	Stromness	11
Cath Clouston	1/449/304	Stromness	25
Margaret Reid	1/460/313	Stromness	20
Barbara Reid	1/460/313	Stromness	19
Mary Reid	1/460/313	Stromness	15
Helen Flett	1/461/313	Stromness	35
Margaret Mowat	1/463/315	Stromness	16
Jannet Louttit	1/467/318	Stromness	20
Margaret Moar	1/474/326	Stromness	15
Ann Mainland	1/475/326	Stromness	20
Christ Mainland	1/475/326	Stromness	14
Christ Archibald	1/481/331	Stromness	14
Margaret Archibald	1/481/331	Stromness	10
Isoble Pottinger	1/482/332	Stromness	25
Isabella Campbell	1/491/337	Stromness	24
Cath Moar	1/497/341	Stromness	20
Eliz Corston	1/500/344	Stromness	19
Ann Corston	1/500/344	Stromness	14
Jean Corston	1/500/344	Stromness	11
Eliz Flett	1/504/348	Stromness	27
Mally Flett	1/504/348	Stromness	18
Jean Michel	1/505/349	Stromness	12
Christ Louttit	1/508/351	Stromness	23
Cath Louttit	1/508/351	Stromness	19
Ann Flett	1/513/354	Stromness	16
Margaret Flett	1/513/354	Stromness	14
Marjory Laughton	1/515/356	Stromness	18
Cath Hunto	1/516/357	Stromness	22
Margaret Harvey	1/517/358	Stromness	23
Margaret Smith	1/524/363	Stromness	17
Eliza Baikie	1/534/369	Stromness	20
Isabella Johnston	1/535/370	Stromness	16

Isabella Clouston	1/542/376 Stromness	14
Christ Clouston	1/542/376 Stromness	11
Cath Johnston	1/547/378 Stromness	28
Catherine Moar	1/555/384 Stromness	35
Jannet Beatton	Clowegarth Kirbister Stromness	21
Ann Dinnet	Haggisback Kirbister Stromness	15
Margaret Clouston	Seater Redland Stromness	20
Eliza Brass	Lower Airean Redland Stromness	21
Ann Brass	Lower Airean Redland Stromness	21
Cath Wilson	Quarrelbanks Redland Stromness	16
Helen Tours	Hall Quholm Stromness	20
Isabella Tours	Hall Quholm Stromness	18
Helen Baikie	Coldholme Quholm Stromness	16
Margaret Baikie	Coldholme Quholm Stromness	14
Ann Baikie	Coldholme Quholm Stromness	11
May Flett	Newhouse Quholm Stromness	20
Eliza Flett	Newhouse Quholm Stromness	16
Ann Belly	Nevishaw Quholm Stromness	24
Jannet Belly	Nevishaw Quholm Stromness	22
Helen Leask	Deepdale Cairston Stromness	20
Marjory Robertson	Whomsley Cairston Stromness	25
Helen Robertson	Whomsley Cairston Stromness	14
Marjory Baikie	Quoybow Cairston Stromness	23
Ann Baikie	Quoybow Cairston Stromness	10
Cath Hourston	Congesquoy Cairston Stromness	18
Margaret Hourston	Congesquoy Cairston Stromness	16
Clemen Brown	Banks Cairston Stromness	14
Eliz Knarston	Little Fea Cairston Stromness	15
Jannet Brass	Snipamira Cairston Stromness	20
Christian Velzian	Holland Cairston Stromness	19
Margaret Wilson	Cothouse Cairston Stromness	38
Sibella Louttit	…apool Cairston Stromness	21
Jannet Clouston	Navishow Cairston Stromness	24
Marjory Thomson	Navishow Cairston Stromness	20
Margaret Thomson	Navishow Cairston Stromness	20
Wilhemina Thomson	Navishow Cairston Stromness	15
Cicilia Hackland	Langhouse Innertown Stromness	40
Euphemia Twatt	W.Breahead Innertown Stromness	31
Jean Moar	Byre Innertown Stromness	36
Ann Moar	Byre Innertown Stromness	30
Jannet Flett	Room Innertown Stromness	41
Jean Flett	Room Innertown Stromness	38
Cath Flett	Room Innertown Stromness	31
Margaret Hunter	Witt Innertown Stromness	24
Cath Hunter	Witt Innertown Stromness	20
May Linklater	Tullochs House Innertown Stromness	18
Cath Wood	Sandyhall Innertown Stromness	24

Margaret Brown	Liefee Innertown Stromness	12
Jannet Brown	Liefee Innertown Stromness	10
Isabella Linklater	Upperhouse Innertown Stromness	35
Allison Linklater	Upperhouse Innertown Stromness	11
Helen Inkster	Chinglebraes Innertown Stromness	40
Ann Inkster	Chinglebraes Innertown Stromness	28
Willamina Byas	Heatherbraes Innertown Stromness	30
Ann Byas	Heatherbraes Innertown Stromness	26
Cath Oman	Upper Pow Innertown Stromness	19
Margaret Moar	Ratter Innertown Stromness	35
Jannet Flett	Quoy of Don Outertown Stromness	15
Jean Irvine	Dykside Outertown Stromness	18
Jannet Flett	Lingmera Outertown Stromness	24
Isabella Flett	Lingmera Outertown Stromness	22
Marjory Flett	Lingmera Outertown Stromness	18
Jannet Flett	Sorquoy Outertown Stromness	15
Cath Flett	Sorquoy Outertown Stromness	10
Ann Forbes	Guart Outertown Stromness	15
Isabella Mowatt	Cot of Dale Outertown Stromness	14
Jannet Thomson	Quoy Anger Outertown Stromness	12
Isabella Moar	Mucklemony Outertown Stromness	15
Jean Irvine	Brockan Outertown Stromness	27
Eliz Sutherland	Upper Bockan Outertown Stromness	17
Jean Davie	Upper Mouseland Stromness	26
Sarah Davie	Upper Mouseland Stromness	23
William Davie	Upper Mouseland Stromness	21
Margaret Davie	Upper Mouseland Stromness	17

1841 Census Records of Strawplaiters

Name	Address	Age	Notes
Margaret Louttit	Palace Birsay	45	
Mary Huntow	Palace Birsay	45	
Ann McDonald	Walkerhouse Birsay	35	
Janet Folster	Walkerhouse Birsay	40	
Margaret Linklater	Walkerhouse Birsay	40	
Mary Adamson	Walkerhouse Birsay	40	
Marion Adamson	Walkerhouse Birsay	35	
Mary Stensgair	Walkerhouse Birsay	20	
Margaret Isbister	Walkerhouse Birsay	60	
Janet Isbister	Walkerhouse Birsay	55	
Eliza Johnston	Walkerhouse Birsay	65	
Ann Huntow	Walkerhouse Birsay	25	
Isabella Spence	Boardhouse Birsay	25	
Mary Spence	Boardhouse Birsay	?	
Hannah Phillips	Langskaill Birsay	35	
Ann Mowat	Breck Birsay	45	
Ann Spence	Glower O'er Birsay	45	
Mary Stenigar	Glower O'er Birsay	15	
Catherine Stenigar	Glower O'er Birsay	15	
Ann Taylor	Glower O'er Birsay	20	
Jean Brown	Breck by South Birsay	30	
Marion Mowat	Barnhouse Birsay	65	
Catherine Sabiston	Grue Birsay	30	
Isabel Mowat	Grue Birsay	40	
Ann Linklater	Harphishay Birsay	55	
Ann Moar	Skedge Birsay	20	
Catherine Johnston	Banks Northside Birsay	35	
Marion Huntlow	Nearhouse Birsay	40	
Mary Johnston	Bathith Birsay	15	
Grizel Johnston	Bathith Birsay	10	
Margaret Folster	Cooperhouse Birsay	30	
Anna Johnston	Gairsty Birsay	20	
Lilian Johnston	Gairsty Birsay	40	
Elizabeth Mowat	Feavale Birsay	50	
Margaret Harvey	Croygec? Birsay	30	
Margaret Spence	Outbrek Birsay	25	
Janet Spence	Outbrek Birsay	20	
Mary Whitelay	Kelday Birsay	40	
Marion Whitelay	Kelday Birsay	33	
Jean Stensgair	Quoys of the Hill Birsay	35	

Janet Stensgair	Quoys of the Hill Birsay	30
Isabells Stensgair	Quoys of the Hill Birsay	25
Cath Moar	Garsetter Birsay	25
Mary Moar	Garsetter Birsay	25
Christian Reeder?	Grindalay Birsay	50
Isabella Johnston	Vindbrek Birsay	30
Isabella Harper	Nervin Birsay	30
Ann Johnston	Wattle Birsay	35
Elisa Moar	Cottages on the hill Birsay	30
Janet Sinclair	Cottages on the hill Birsay	50
Margaret Sinclair	Cottages on the hill Birsay	25
Frances Sinclair	Cottages on the hill Birsay	25
Isabella Spence	Park Birsay	40
Margaret Harvey	Park Birsay	45
Mary Spence	Banks Birsay	35
Mary Spence	Banks Birsay	45
? Spence	Quoys Birsay	30
Mary Spence	Istabist Birsay	20
Ann Johnston	Millbrig Birsay	40
Margaret Linklater	Lochend Birsay	50
Margaret Mowat	Twatt Birsay	40
Margaret Mowat	Twatt Birsay	15
Mary Spence	Twatt Birsay	40
Mehetabel Harvey	Greeny Birsay	25
Francis Harvey	Greeny Birsay	15
Mary Spence	Greeny Birsay	25
Mary Garson	Greeny Birsay	30
Achsa? Smith	Greeny Birsay	30
Mary Rowland	Greeny Birsay	30
Margaret Spence	Greeny Birsay	50
Margaret Spence	Greeny Birsay	20
Sibella Harvey	Greeny Birsay	20
Ann Merriman	Greeny Birsay	20
Mary Kirkness	Greeny Birsay	15
Margaret Kirkness	Greeny Birsay	15
Mary Merriman	Greeny Birsay	35
Catherine Spence	Greeny Birsay	15
Ann Spence	Greeny Birsay	15
Leah Swordie	Greeny Birsay	30
Elizabeth Johnston	Greeny Birsay	20
Janet Harvey	Greeny Birsay	50
Janet Harvey	Greeny Birsay	15
Elizabeth Harvey	Greeny Birsay	20
Ann Isbister	Greeny Birsay	13
Margaret Linklater	Sabiston Birsay	35
Ann Linklater	Sabiston Birsay	20
Margaret Linklater	Sabiston Birsay	15

Shusan? Clouston	Sabiston Birsay	15
Elizabeth Flett	Sabiston Birsay	40
Mary Anderson	Sabiston Birsay	35
Ann Merriman	Sabiston Birsay	35
Catherine Mowat	Sabiston Birsay	30
Betty Mowat	Sabiston Birsay	20
Catherine Flett	Sabiston Birsay	35
Margaret Flett	Sabiston Birsay	35
Mary Flett	Sabiston Birsay	30
Hannah Firth	Sabiston Birsay	50
Janet Flett	Beaquoy Birsay	20
Margaret Miller	Beaquoy Birsay	35
Ann Johnston	Beaquoy Birsay	20
Maria Johnston	Beaquoy Birsay	20
Mary Mowat	Beaquoy Birsay	20
Janet Mowat	Beaquoy Birsay	15
Ann Merriman	Beaquoy Birsay	20
Janet Merriman	Beaquoy Birsay	15
Mary Marwick	Beaquoy Birsay	15
Margaret Johnston	Isbister Birsay	25
Jean Scarth	Isbister Birsay	20
Margaret Kirkness	Isbister Birsay	10
Catherine Ritch	Isbister Birsay	30
Mary Ritch	Isbister Birsay	25
Mary Breck	Marwick Birsay	25
Margret Moar	Marwick Birsay	30
Ann Stickler	Marwick Birsay	40
Ann Stickler	Marwick Birsay	8
Mary Spence	Marwick Birsay	65
Jean Taylor	Marwick Birsay	20
Jean Mowat	Marwick Birsay	55
Elizabeth Louttit	Marwick Birsay	60
Isabella Stanger	Marwick Birsay	20
Elizabeth Stanger	Marwick Birsay	20
?Taylor	Marwick Birsay	30
?Gaudie	Marwick Birsay	35
Isabella Stickler	Marwick Birsay	35
Ann Breck	Marwick Birsay	25
Janet Breck	Marwick Birsay	20
Marrion Taylor	Marwick Birsay	35
Elizabeth Taylor	Marwick Birsay	20
Eupehmia Matches	Pictil Deerness	30
Sarah Foulis	Noutland Deerness	40
Jane Finnison	New Schoolhouse Deerness	30
Jane Linklater	Jameshouse Deerness	50
Margaret Harcus	Burraquoy Hall Deerness	35
Jane Skea	I. Schoolhouse Deerness	30

Ann Flett	Belquoy Deerness	20	
Margaret Ritch	Babylon Deerness	25	
Elizabeth Aitken	Pickletilium Deerness	35	
Ellen Paplay	Little Colster Deerness	35	
Jane Foubister	Trotties Deerness	20	
Margaret Stove	Little Millhouse Deerness	40	
Margaret Reid	Gairsty Deerness	20	
Ann Banks	Little Quoys Deerness	40	
Elizabeth Tait	Ploverhall Deerness	25	
Jane Dunnet	Little Esnaphy Deerness	35	
Ann Mowat	Silordyke Deerness	30	
Margaret Esson	Brandiquoy Deerness	25	
Mary Esson	Brandiquoy Deerness	35	
Margaret Smith	Queenanea Deerness	35	
Ann Smith	Queenanea Deerness	30	
Ann Stove	Barebreck Deerness	15	
Isabella Stove	Barebreck Deerness	14	
Ann Stove	Barebreck Deerness	40	
Sophie Ritch	South Skea Deerness	15	
Margaret Foulis	Horraquoy Deerness	35	
Catherine Foulis	Horraquoy Deerness	30	
Mary Kirkness	Copinsay	15	
Jennet Harcus	Eday NW Lodge	50	
Elizabeth Spence	Eday NW Newbigging	40	
Margaret Shearer	Eday SE Hungrihaw	20	
Mary Reid	Eday SE Banke	20	straw bonnet maker
Barbara Reid	Eday SE Banke	15	
Jean Rousay	Eday SE Dykside	20	
Margaret Reid	Eday SE Groathaw	15	house servant
Barbara Cormack	Eday SE Blackbanks	20	married 1841
Isabella Cormack	Eday SE Blackbanks	15	married 1843
Jean Scott	Eday SE Mounthoolie	20	married 1846
Ann Reid	Eday SE Manseboat	15	
Jean Reid	Eday SE Loughend	15	
Christian Flett	Slap Evie	25	
Margaret Anderson	Idnager Evie	25	
Betsy Hourston	Burnbraes Evie	35	
Ann Hourston	Burnbraes Evie	35	
January Yorston	Akerness Evie	35	
Mary Marwick	Newhouse Evie	40	
Ann Hourston	North End Rendall	35	manufacturer of plaits
Betty Robertson	North End Rendall	35	manufacturer of plaits
Mary Marwick	Isbister Rendall	30	
Ann Slater	Isbister Rendall	25	
Barbara Borwick	Halkland Rendall	25	
Janet Mathieson	Braigar Rendall	25	
Mary Rendall	Cottisgarth Rendall	25	

118

Barbara Hourston	Gairsay	30	
Betty Grieve	Gairsay	30	
Ann Bichan	Gairsay	55	
Mary Horie	Settescarth Firth	25	
Jane Slatter	Settescarth Firth	40	
Elspet Scletter	Redland Firth	55	
Christiana Hourie	Redland Firth	40	
Margaret Yorston	Redland Firth	45	
Mary Corrigal	Redland Firth	40	
Margaret Louttit	Holland Firth	13	
Catherine Flett	Holland Firth	30	
Catherine Jack	Horraldshay Firth	55	
Mary Harray	Horraldshay Firth	25	
Isabella Harray	Horraldshay Firth	20	straw bonnet maker
Margaret Flett	Snaba Firth	19	
Jean Flett	Snaba Firth	17	
Cicila Firth	Snaba Firth	45	
Margaret Leith	Snaba Firth	20	
Catherine Firth	Wasdale Firth	40	
Ann Sinclair	Binscarth Firth	13	
Cicilia Wilson	Thickbigging Firth	35	
Jean Flett	Cursiter Firth	30	
Catherine Swanson	Cursiter Firth	20	
Catherine Flett	Grimbister Firth	40	
Mary Flett	Fettercairn Stenness	20	
Jean Flett	Fettercairn Stenness	20	
Sibilla Corrigall	Northbiggin Harray	20	
Elizabeth Linklater	Holodyke Harray	15	
Elizabeth Linklater	Holodyke Harray	40	
Margaret Hay	Mithower Harray	20	
Betsy Hay	Mithower Harray	20	
Margaret Stanger	Mithouse Harray	55	
Jean Hay	Mithouse Harray	15	
Mary Baikie	Mountera Harray	25	married? Nee Scott
Mary Hourston	London Harray	15	
Jean Hourston	London Harray	5	
Jean Linklater	Breckan Harray	30	
Janet King	How o Dilly Harray	25	
May Johnstone	Bretovale Harray	20	
Margaret Johnstone	Bretovale Harray	15	
Jean Johnstone	Bretovale Harray	14	
Ann Isbister	Nether Gueth Harray	20	
Margaret Flett	Nistaben Harray	20	
Ann Flett	Nistaben Harray	15	
Ann Hourston	Hozen Harray	25	
Margaret Hourston	Hozen Harray	20	
Catherine Hourston	Hozen Harray	20	

Mary Hourston	Hozen Harray	15	
Janet Flett	Whilkur ? Harray	20	
Jean Flett	Whilkur ? Harray	15	
Ann Miller	Whilkur ? Harray	25	married? Nee Flett
Mary Linklater	Outadkyes Harray	30	
Betsy Kirkness	Kingshouse Harray	10	
Sybella Flett	Kingshouse Harray	20	
Margaret Flett	Kingshouse Harray	15	
Margaret Smith	Garth Harray	15	
Marjory Clouston	Garth Harray	35	
Betsy Kenyon	Garth Harray	20	
Ann Kirkness	Nether Corston Harray	10	
Jane Spence	Bridge Scuan Harray	10	
Marjory Harper	Hurries Harray	55	
Betty Scott	Quina Harray	35	
Jane Scott	Quina Harray	25	
Catherine Robertson	Moan Harray	25	
Isabella Robertson	Biggins Harray	15	
Jean Robertson	Biggins Harray	25	
Margaret Robertson	Biggins Harray	30	
Elizabeth Sinclair	Conyer Harray	45	
Margaret Hourston	Thwartgreen Harray	11	
Margaret Smith	Gairth Harray	15	
Ann Corrigall	Bliest Harray	25	
Sibbla Corrigall	Bliest Harray	20	
Margaret Merriman	Maesquoy Harray	15	
Mary Corrigall	Pow Harray	15	
Sybella Sinclair	Overbrough Harray	25	
Barbara Sinclair	Overbrough Harray	20	
May Sinclair	Overbrough Harray	15	
Helen Borwick	Nisthouse Harray	20	
Margaret Kirkness	Moan Harray	30	
Helen Kirkness	Moan Harray	20	
Mary Kirkness	Moan Harray	25	
Jean Kirkness	Cuppin Harray	15	
Ann Merriman	Nether Appietoun Harray	13	
Catherine Corrigall	Outhouse Harray	40	
Margaret Corrigall	Outhouse Harray	25	
Helen Flett	Midnatoon Harray	20	
Catherine Johnstone	Midnatoon Harray	55	
Mary Sinclair	Midnatoon Harray	30	
Isabella Smith	Tevath Harray	15	
Helen Flett	Bluthamo Harray	30	
Christina Flett	Bluthamo Harray	25	
Isabella Johnstone	Quina Harray	30	
Barbara Johnstone	Quina Harray	20	
Christian Flett	Lammaquoy Harray	55	

Margaret Flett	Lammaquoy Harray	50
Margaret Manson	Stripol Harray	30
Elizabeth Manson	Stripol Harray	30
Sibella Manson	Stripol Harray	20
Helen Manson	Stripol Harray	20
Betty Manson	Stripol Harray	15
Jean Manson	Stripol Harray	15
Isabella Kirkness	Gyron Harray	50
Mary Smith	Garth Harray	20
Betty Smith	Garth Harray	15
Margaret Smith	Garth Harray	15
Jean Smith	Garth Harray	15
Ann Smith	Nethergarth Harray	40
Mary Smith	Bow Harray	20
Jean Merriman	Eastaquoy Harray	25
Margaret Merriman	Eastaquoy Harray	15
Ann Kirkness	Geroin Harray	50
Jean Kirkness	Upper Hunscarth Harray	15
Mary Flett	Nether Hunscarth Harray	15
Jean Murray	Granawan Harray	30
Helen Sinclair	Granawan Harray	40
Helen Louttit	Nettletar Harray	25
Ann Firth	Nettletar Harray	40
Mary Firth	Nettletar Harray	35
Margaret Merriman	Nether Howe Harray	11
Elizabeth Linklater	Queer Harray	40
Isabella Corrigall	Upper Howe Harray	40
Betty Kirkness	Howe Harray	20
Jean Kirkness	Howe Harray	15
Ann Borwick	Howe Harray	30
Ann Corrigall	Geroin Harray	25
Isabella Corrigall	Geroin Harray	15
Jean Isbister	Oback Harray	15
Betty Isbister	Oback Harray	14
Isabella Isbister	Oback Harray	11
Catherine Moar	Meiron Harray	15
Mary Moar	Meiron Harray	12
Peggy Clouston	Meiron Harray	20
Isabella Clouston	Meiron Harray	15
Margaret Johnstone	Quoykea Harray	35
Mary Johnstone	Quoykea Harray	30
Margaret Velzian	AppieHouse Harray	15
Mary Velzian	AppieHouse Harray	13
Margaret Flett	Nisthousc Harray	15
Mary Smith	Bews,Bewhouse Harray	20
Betty Anderson	Appiehouse Harray	35
Christian Anderson	AppieHouse Harray	25

Betty Spence	Beckan Harray	15	
Margaret Isbister	Nearhouse Harray	25	
Christian Scott	Fursbeck Harray	45	
Betty Corrigall	Nearhouse Harray	15	
Marjory Kirkness	Nearhouse Harray	40	
Margaret Clouston	Nearhouse Harray	60	
Margery Clouston	Breck Harray	40	married? Nee Scott
Margaret Scott	Beneath Dyke Harray	20	
Marjory Brown	Windywalls Harray	40	
Christian Brown	Windywalls Harray	35	
Mary Corrigall	Skiirpaquoy Harray	13	
Margaret Russland	Skiirpaquoy Harray	30	straw hat maker
Jane Kirkness	Nistaben Harray	20	
Betty Flett	Vola Harray	15	
Bettly Redland	Vola Harray	35	
Isabella Johnstone	Biggins Harray	12	
Mary Isbister	Queenafinya Harray	20	
Helen Isbister	Queenafinya Harray	15	
Jennet Thomson	Cot Hoy	33	
Kaithren Mowat	A Chamber Hoy	30	
Mary Mowat	Bennalhall Hoy	20	
Jean Mowat	Bennalhall Hoy	15	
Ann Lyon	A Chamber Hoy	55	
Isabella Linklater	A Chamber Hoy	14	
Ann Mowat	A Chamber Hoy	35	
Marget Oman	Upper Quoys Hoy	15	
Ann Oman	Upper Quoys Hoy	14	
Isabella Green	Manabreak Hoy	14	
Margaret ?	A Chamber Hoy	40	
Margret Young	Winbreak Hoy	25	
Jannet Young	Winbreak Hoy	15	
Hellen Young	Winbreak Hoy	20	
Kaithreen Lyon	Clett Hoy	15	
Jean Lyon	Clett Hoy	14	
Helen Robertson	Wellington St Kirkwall	65	
Isabella Garrioch	Wellington St Kirkwall	50	
Barbara MacKay	Wellington St Kirkwall	15	
Janet MacDonald	Wellington St Kirkwall	20	
Janet Spence	Wellington St Kirkwall	30	
Catherine Wilson	Wellington St Kirkwall	75	
Isabella Watt	Wellington St Kirkwall	40	
Margaret Taylor	Wellington St Kirkwall	25	
Janet Wilson	Wellington St Kirkwall	50	b. Scotland
Catherine Wilson	Wellington St Kirkwall	35	
Ann Gunn	Wellington St Kirkwall	50	
Ann Beatton	Wellington St Kirkwall	20	
Ann Heddle	Wellington St Kirkwall	40	or Work?

Margaret Heddle	Wellington St Kirkwall	40	
Elizabeth McLellan	Wellington St Kirkwall	45	
Christian Sutherland	Wellington St Kirkwall	25	
Mary Bews	Wellington St Kirkwall	50	
Margaret McDonald	Wellington St Kirkwall	50	
Margaret McDonald	Wellington St Kirkwall	14	
Catharine Miller	Wellington St Kirkwall	45	
John Ballantyne	Wellington St Kirkwall		b 1766
Janet Chalmers	Wellington St Kirkwall	60	
Margaret Marwick	Wellington St Kirkwall	50	
Christiana Tait	Main St Kirkwall	40	
Margaret Tulloch	Main St Kirkwall	60	
Margaret Watt	Main St Kirkwall	35	
Margaret Matheson	Main St Kirkwall	15	
Isabella Farquhar	Main St Kirkwall	40	
Amelia Greig	Main St Kirkwall	50	
Wilhemina Anderson	Main St Kirkwall	40	
Ann Moodie	Main St Kirkwall	40	
Barbara Peace	Main St Kirkwall	80	
Eliza Warren	Main St Kirkwall	20	
Elizabeth Voy	Main St Kirkwall	45	
Barbara Voy	Main St Kirkwall	40	
Ann Heddle	Main St Kirkwall	55	
Margaret Heddle	Main St Kirkwall	20	
Jean Hourie	Main St Kirkwall	55	
Stewart Rendall (F)	Main St Kirkwall	25	
Sarah Spence	Main St Kirkwall	15	
Ann Tulloch	Union St Kirkwall	25	bonnet maker
Catherine Garrioch	Union St Kirkwall	20	bonnet maker
May Louttit	Union St Kirkwall	45	
Barbara Groundwater	Victoria St Kirkwall	60	
Catharine Flett	Victoria St Kirkwall	45	
Janet Flett	Victoria St Kirkwall	40	
Elizabeth Groundwater	Victoria St Kirkwall	40	bonnet maker
Janet McLellan	Victoria St Kirkwall	25	
Mary Slater	Victoria St Kirkwall	15	bonnet maker
Mary Holland	Victoria St Kirkwall	50	Leghorn sewer
Mary Laughton	Victoria St Kirkwall	20	
Jean Gorrie	Victoria St Kirkwall	40	
Margaret Flaws	Victoria St Kirkwall	40	
Catherine Corston	Victoria Rd Kirkwall	55	straw plait dresser
Jean Tait	Victoria Rd Kirkwall	40	straw hat maker
Betsy Tait	Victoria Rd Kirkwall	35	straw hat maker
Betty Chalmers	Victoria Rd Kirkwall	55	
Mary Guthrie	Victoria Rd Kirkwall	25	
Janet Harper	Victoria St Kirkwall	40	
Margaret Holland	Victoria St Kirkwall	45	

Margaret Holland	Victoria St Kirkwall	15	
Helen Shearer	Victoria St Kirkwall	35	Leghorn Bonnet maker
Jean Fotheringhame	Victoria St Kirkwall	40	
Margaret Fotheringhame	Victoria St Kirkwall	35	
Betsy Christie	Victoria St Kirkwall	50	
Jean Christie	Victoria St Kirkwall	15	
Georgina Christie	Victoria St Kirkwall	15	
Barbara Laird	Victoria St Kirkwall	40	
Barbara Laird	Victoria St Kirkwall	20	
Stewart Laird (F)	Victoria St Kirkwall	15	
Mary Bichan	Victoria St Kirkwall	20	
Barbara James	Victoria St Kirkwall	55	sizer of straw
Barbara James	Victoria St Kirkwall	15	
Margaret Harrold	Victoria St Kirkwall	20	
Margaret Holland	Victoria St Kirkwall	20	bonnet maker
Mary Wallace	Victoria St Kirkwall	55	Leghorn sewer
Mary Wallace	Victoria St Kirkwall	35	Leghorn sewer
Jane Wallace	Victoria St Kirkwall	25	Leghorn sewer
Ann Wallace	Victoria St Kirkwall	20	Leghorn sewer
Ann Garrioch	Victoria St Kirkwall	40	
Mary Mowat	Victoria St Kirkwall	50	straw plait manufacturer
Sohia Craigie	Victoria St Kirkwall	35	
Isabella Petrie	Victoria St Kirkwall	20	
Margaret Ross	Victoria St Kirkwall	60	
Jean Banker	Victoria St Kirkwall	20	bonnet maker
Margaret Moir	Victoria St Kirkwall	35	
Rebecca Tulloch	Victoria St Kirkwall	20	
Euphemia Keldy	Victoria St Kirkwall	60	
Sibilla Gray	Victoria St Kirkwall	40	straw cleaner
Mary Foubister	Victoria St Kirkwall	30	hat maker
Euphemia Finlayson	Victoria St Kirkwall	40	
Isabella Foulis	Victoria St Kirkwall	25	straw hat maker
Barbara Gorie	Victoria St Kirkwall	60	
Nancy Miller	Victoria St Kirkwall	60	
Isabella Miller	Victoria St Kirkwall	75	straw cutter
Isabella Manson	Victoria St Kirkwall	20	bonnet maker
Margaret Kirkness	Victoria St Kirkwall	50	
Margaret Kirkness	Victoria St Kirkwall	20	
Barbara Kirkness	Victoria St Kirkwall	20	
Mary Gaudie	Victoria St Kirkwall	65	straw cutter (Marion?)
Margaret Sutherland	Victoria St Kirkwall	20	bonnet sewer
Mary Sutherland	Victoria St Kirkwall	20	
Ann Sutherland	Victoria St Kirkwall	15	
Elizabeth Sutherland	Victoria St Kirkwall	12	
Janet Learmonth	Victoria St Kirkwall	40	
Margaret Williamson	Victoria St Kirkwall	25	bonnet maker
Isabella Leask	Victoria St Kirkwall	15	bonnet maker

Jane Miller	Victoria St Kirkwall	45	
Robina Erskine	Victoria St Kirkwall	15	straw hat maker
Barbara Mainland	Broad St Kirkwall	45	straw manufacturer
Jane Elrick	Broad St Kirkwall	15	
Margaret Smith	Broad St Kirkwall	20	straw hat maker
Mary Smith	Broad St Kirkwall	40	
Margaret Voy	Strand Kirkwall	60	
Margaret Ferguson	Strand Kirkwall	15	
Ann Smith	Strand Kirkwall	15	
Ellen Mitchel	Albert St Kirkwall	40	
Janet Allan	Albert St Kirkwall	20	
Margaret Scott	Albert St Kirkwall	50	
Jean Chalmers	Albert St Kirkwall	50	
Mary Innis	Albert St Kirkwall	60	
Catherine Baikie	Albert St Kirkwall	25	
Jean Seater	Albert St Kirkwall	35	
Isabella Muir	Albert St Kirkwall	15	
Catharine Tait	Albert St Kirkwall	40	
Elizabeth Peace	Albert St Kirkwall	55	
Janet Scott	Albert St Kirkwall	45	
Margaret Wilson	Albert St Kirkwall	40	
Eliza Clouston	Albert St Kirkwall	30	
Grace Clouston	Albert St Kirkwall	25	
Jane Johnston	Albert Lane Kirkwall	25	
Elizabeth Corse	Albert Lane Kirkwall	14	
Mary Walls	Albert Lane Kirkwall	40	
Jane Flett	Albert Lane Kirkwall	20	
Janet Dearness	Albert Lane Kirkwall	60	
Jean Dearness	Albert Lane Kirkwall	55	
Mary Dearness	Albert Lane Kirkwall	70	
Mary Heddle	Bridge St Kirkwall	25	
Betsy Tourie	Bridge St Kirkwall	20	
Barbara Flett	Bridge St Kirkwall	60	
Margaret Chalmers	Bridge St Kirkwall	20	straw bonnet maker
Barbara Alexander	Bridge St Kirkwall	45	
Margaret Drever	Bridge St Kirkwall	20	
Catherine Drever	Bridge St Kirkwall	15	
Elizabeth Reid	Bridge St Lane Kirkwall	50	
Mary Reid	Bridge St Lane Kirkwall	25	bonnet maker
Janet Muir	Bridge St Kirkwall	35	married nee Linay
Mary Muir	Bridge St Kirkwall	55	
Janet Garson	Bridge Wynd Kirkwall	50	
Barbara Peace	Bridge Wynd Kirkwall	20	
Jean Peace	Bridge Wynd Kirkwall	20	
Isabella Irvine	Bridge Wynd Kirkwall	20	straw bonnet maker
Elizabeth Irvine	Bridge Wynd Kirkwall	15	straw bonnet maker
Christian Harrold	Albert St Kirkwall	20	

Margaret McSwanney	Albert St Kirkwall	15	straw bonnet maker
Helen Swanay	Albert St Kirkwall	50	
George McBeath	Albert St Kirkwall	40	straw hat manufacturer b. Scotland
Joshua Robertson	Albert St Kirkwall	20	shopman
Barbara Maxwell	Harbour St Kirkwall	65	straw oiler
Robina Wick	Harbour St Kirkwall	25	
Isabella Wick	Harbour St Kirkwall	25	
Lydia Scarth	Shore St Kirkwall	35	
Anne Turnbull	Shore St Kirkwall	25	bonnet maker
Ann Work	Shore St Kirkwall	40	
Mary Sclater	Shore St Kirkwall	20	
Jean Sclater	Shore St Kirkwall	20	
Janet Mainland	Shore St Kirkwall	60	
Catharine Skea	Shore St Kirkwall	30	
Mary Low	Shore St Kirkwall	12	
Elizabeth Small	Shore St Kirkwall	55	
Jean Waller?	Shore St Kirkwall	20	
Barbara Bichan	Shore St Kirkwall	30	
Anne Montgomery	Shore St Kirkwall	50	
Anne Montgomery	Shore St Kirkwall	10	
Janet Flaws	Shore St Kirkwall	55	
Grace Sinclair	Shore St Kirkwall	45	
Christian Sinclair	Shore St Kirkwall	20	
Janet Chambers	Shore St Kirkwall	25	
Mary Guthrie	Shore St Kirkwall	30	
Anne Guthrie	Shore St Kirkwall	25	
Margaret Corrigall	Shore St Kirkwall	60	
Betsy Corsie	Shore St Kirkwall	30	
Mary Craigie	Shore St Kirkwall	15	
Mary Flett	Shore St Kirkwall	15	
Mary Cooper	Shore St Kirkwall	55	
Janet Finnison	Shore St Kirkwall	20	
Jean Petrie	Shore St Kirkwall	30	
Margaret Goar	Shore St Kirkwall	25	
Jean Goar	Shore St Kirkwall	20	
Barbara Mitchell	Shore St Kirkwall	20	
Mary Harvey	Shore St Kirkwall	15	
Janet Thompson	Shore St Kirkwall	25	
Catharine Miller	Long Wynd Kirkwall	45	
Jane Sinclair	Long Wynd Kirkwall	35	
Janet Miller	Long Wynd Kirkwall	15	
Anne Craigie	Long Wynd Kirkwall	25	
Margaret Croy	Long Wynd Kirkwall	35	
Mary Sclater	Long Wynd Kirkwall	40	
Margaret Walls	Long Wynd Kirkwall	50	
Isabella Spence	Long Wynd Kirkwall	45	

Jean Dinnison	Long Wynd Kirkwall	15	
Anne Driver	Long Wynd Kirkwall	25	
Margaret Jones	Long Wynd Kirkwall	55	
Mary Jones	Long Wynd Kirkwall	20	
Barbara Muir	Long Wynd Kirkwall	40	
Anne Reid	Long Wynd Kirkwall	30	
Helen Bews	Long Wynd Kirkwall	40	
Elizabeth Fairweather	Long Wynd Kirkwall	35	
Mary Fairweather	Long Wynd Kirkwall	30	
Janet Dearness	Long Wynd Kirkwall	15	
Mary Ann Peace	Long Wynd Kirkwall	20	
Barbara Bews	Long Wynd Kirkwall	45	
Mary Bews	Long Wynd Kirkwall	20	bonnet maker
Barbara Sclater	Shore St Kirkwall	30	
Janet Scott	Shore St Kirkwall	40	
Isabella Hutchison	Shore St Kirkwall	40	
Janet Fairweather	Shore St Kirkwall	35	
Margaret Rendall	Shore St Kirkwall	20	
Jean Ross	Nicolson St Kirkwall	15	
Barbara Calder	High St Kirkwall	20	
Jean Wilson	High St Kirkwall	15	
Jean Heddle	High St Kirkwall	15	
Mary Heddle	High St Kirkwall	14	
Margaret Chalmers	High St Kirkwall	60	
Ann Clouston	High St Kirkwall	50	
Jean Clouston	High St Kirkwall	20	hat draper
Ann Cooper	High St Kirkwall	50	
Catherine Robertson	High St Kirkwall	55	
Catherine Robertson	High St Kirkwall	30	
Barbara Robertson	High St Kirkwall	20	
Marjory Craigie	High St Kirkwall	60	
Sarah Linklater	High St Kirkwall	55	
Jessie Linklater	High St Kirkwall	20	
Mary Dick	High St Kirkwall	45	
Mary Hepburn	High St Kirkwall	25	
Ann Eunson	High St Kirkwall	50	
Margaret Eunson	High St Kirkwall	60	
Margaret Leask	High St Kirkwall	45	
Margaret Leask	High St Kirkwall	20	
Helen Wilson	High St Kirkwall	65	
James Gray	High St Kirkwall	60	
Ann Peace	High St Kirkwall	55	
Mary Peace	High St Kirkwall	45	
Barbara Groundwater	High St Kirkwall	60	
Barbara Groundwater	High St Kirkwall	20	
Mary Thompson	Union St Kirkwall	30	
Margaret Peace	Union St Kirkwall	60	

Betsy Sinclair	Back St Kirkwall	15	
Catherine Sinclair	Back St Kirkwall	30	
Betsy Sinclair	Back St Kirkwall	20	
Helen Sinclair	Back St Kirkwall	15	
Betsy Muir	Back St Kirkwall	20	
Isabella Hollan?	Back St Kirkwall	35	
Margaret Heddle	Back St Kirkwall	15	
Betsy Drever	Back Road Kirkwall	40	
Jean Peace	School Place Kirkwall	30	
Helen Linklater	School Place Kirkwall	40	
Mary Linklater	School Place Kirkwall	25	
Helen Maxwell	School Place Kirkwall	55	
Christian Eunson	School Place Kirkwall	20	
Nancy Dearness	School Place Kirkwall	30	
Margaret Smith	School Place Kirkwall	45	
Barbara Smith	School Place Kirkwall	30	
Rebecca Smith	School Place Kirkwall	25	
Betsy Clouston	School Place Kirkwall	60	
Ann Malcolm	School Place Kirkwall	40	
Ann Hepburn	Union St Kirkwall	25	
Mary Johnston	Millhouse Kirkwall	25	bonnet maker
Ann Flett	Mill St Kirkwall	15	
Mary Flett	Mill St Kirkwall	14	
Margaret Linnay	Mill St Kirkwall	15	
Isabella Shearer	Mill St Kirkwall	14	
May Ritch	Mill St Kirkwall	13	
Elizabeth Sclatter	Queen St Kirkwall	30	straw bonnet maker
Jennet Scott	Queen St Kirkwall	35	
Barbara Guthrie	Queen St Kirkwall	40	
Ann Learmouth	Queen St Kirkwall	14	
Margaret Eunson	Queen St Kirkwall	14	
Ann Linklater	Queen St Kirkwall	40	
Margaret Muir	Queen St Kirkwall	25	
Elizabeth Muir	Queen St Kirkwall	15	
Barbra Leask	Queen St Kirkwall	30	
David Ramsay	Queen St Kirkwall	60	straw plait manufacturer b. Scotland
Marget Spence	East Road Kirkwall	20	straw bonnet maker
Mary Wards	East Road Kirkwall	45	married nee Marwick
Isabella Wards	East Road Kirkwall	15	
Hellen Wards	East Road Kirkwall	12	
Sarah Wards	East Road Kirkwall	10	
Jean Wards	East Road Kirkwall	14	
Margret Brodie	Farm of Weyland Kirkwall	15	
Mary Brodie	Farm of Weyland Kirkwall	15	
Betsy Brodie	Farm of Weyland Kirkwall	15	
Ann Hunter	Catherine Place Kirkwall	40	

Frances Grive	Catherine Place Kirkwall	15	
Jennet Muir	Catherine Place Kirkwall	20	
Barbra Muir	Catherine Place Kirkwall	15	
Ann Innes	Catherine Place Kirkwall	30	
Jessie Hourston	Catherine Place Kirkwall	40	seaman's wife
Margret Muir	Catherine Place Kirkwall	15	
Margret Muir	Catherine Place Kirkwall	25	
Mary Drever	Catherine Place Kirkwall	15	
Margret Matches	Catherine Place Kirkwall	55	
Margret Petrie	Catherine Place Kirkwall	15	
Elizabeth Millar	Catherine Place Kirkwall	50	
Jean Reid	Catherine Place Kirkwall	20	
Barbra Irvine	Catherine Place Kirkwall	11	
William Bews	Catherine Place Kirkwall	20	straw sorter
Margret Bews	Catherine Place Kirkwall	15	
Betty Hourston	Catherine Place Kirkwall	25	
Margret Hourston	Catherine Place Kirkwall	20	
Elisabeth Garrioch	Catherine Place Kirkwall	15	
Jane Garrioch	Catherine Place Kirkwall	15	
Barbra Garrioch	Catherine Place Kirkwall	12	
Jean Angus	Catherine Place Kirkwall	45	
Jean Angus	Catherine Place Kirkwall	14	
Margret Angus	Catherine Place Kirkwall	12	
Mary Dearness	Catherine Place Kirkwall	40	
Hellen Brodie	Catherine Place Kirkwall	35	
Isabella Scott	Catherine Place Kirkwall	45	
Ellenor Scott	Catherine Place Kirkwall	20	
Mary Chalson	Catherine Place Kirkwall	55	
Elisabeth Scott	Catherine Place Kirkwall	25	
Mary Ann Michell	Young St Kirkwall	40	
Jennet Fowles	Young St Kirkwall	30	
Eliza Cameron	Young St Kirkwall	55	
Mary Groundwater	Young St Kirkwall	20	
Jean Millar	Catherine Place Kirkwall	50	
Bettsy Cooper	Catherine Place Kirkwall	25	
Isabella Bruce	Catherine Place Kirkwall	9	
Margret Drever	Catherine Place Kirkwall	50	
Barbara Dinison	Seater Kirkwall	30	
Jean Leask	South Cott, Caldale Kirkwall	50	
Margaret G Bremner	Lower Caldale Kirkwall	35	
Jessie Bremner	Lower Caldale Kirkwall	14	
Willamina Bremner	Lower Caldale Kirkwall	12	
Ceclia Smith	1.1. Orphir	25	
Margaret Smith	1.1 Orphir	25	
Mary Sinclair	1.8 Orphir	30	
Betty Sinclair	1.8 Orphir	25	
Margaret Sinclair	1.9 Orphir	35	

Margaret Moncrieff	1.9 Orphir	15	
Williamina Moncrieff	1.9 Orphir	13	
Christian Murray	1.12 Orphir	45	
Catherine Halcrow	1.15 Orphir	40	
Catherine Linklater	1.19 Orphir	60	
Janet Sclater	1.34 Orphir	25	
Christian Sclater	1.34 Orphir	25	
Margaret Sinclair	1.36 Orphir	40	nee Loutit
Jessie Sinclair	1.36 Orphir	15	
Catherine Sinclair	1.40 Orphir	40	
Margaret Tait	1.48 Orphir	25	
Ann Tait	1.48 Orphir	15	
Catherine Garriock	1.52 Orphir	55	
Margaret Inkster	2.1 Orphir	20	
Barbara Johnston	2.8 Orphir	30	
Margaret Groundwater	2.14 Orphir	20	
Ann Taylor	2.16 Orphir	25	
Jean Nicolson	2.17 Orphir	40	
Ann Hutchison	2.17 Orphir	50	
Ann Flett	2.48 Orphir	40	
Margaret Flett	2.48 Orphir	35	
Jannet Leask	2.50 Orphir	40	
Mary Davidson	2.50 Orphir	20	
Christian Taylor	3.19 Orphir	25	
Jean Taylor	3.19 Orphir	20	
Barbara Sletter	3.24 Orphir	20	
Betty Sletter	3.24 Orphir	25	
Effy Ballantine	3.27 Orphir	35	
Mary Loutit	4.3 Orphir	25	
Ann Loutit	4.3 Orphir	25	
Margaret Loutit	4.3 Orphir	20	
Elizabeth Loutit	4.3 Orphir	20	
Margaret Flett	4.10 Orphir	40	
Cecilia Hay	4.23 Orphir	75	
Christian Corner	5.4 Orphir	25	
Hellen Corner	5.4 Orphir	20	
Phebe Corner	5.4 Orphir	20	
Margaret Friker?	5.5 Orphir	35	
Christian Ballantine	5.7 Orphir	30	
Mary Tait	5.10 Orphir	20	
Isabella Taylor	5.14 Orphir	20	
Katherine Taylor	5.14 Orphir	15	
Ann Sinclair	5.18 Orphir	20	
Hanna Leask	5.23 Orphir	25	
Inga Johnston	5.30 Orphir	25	
Catherine Johnston	5.30 Orphir	20	
Betty Finlay	5.31 Orphir	25	

Jane Finlay	5.31 Orphir	20	
Cecilia Finlay	5.31 Orphir	15	
Katharine Robertson	5.34 Orphir	50	
Margaret Flett	5.34 Orphir	20	
Jean Flett	5.34 Orphir	20	
Katherine Flett	5.34 Orphir	15	
Jean Manson	6.7 Orphir	25	
Margaret Manson	6.7 Orphir	20	
Isabella Manson	6.7 Orphir	20	
Helen Robertson	6.11 Orphir	20	
Jane Garriock	6.12 Orphir	50	
Jane Liney	6.14 Orphir	40	
Margaret Liney	6.14 Orphir	35	
Margaret Liney	6.14 Orphir	15	
Barbara Flett	6.16 Orphir	25	
Ann Flett	6.16 Orphir	20	
Betsy Craigie	Quoyfaro Rousay	30	
Julia Mainland	Nethermill Rousay	25	bonnet maker
Margaret Craigie	2/1 unrecorded Rousay	15	
Robina Marwick	2/9 Unrecorded Rousay	20	
Isabella Marwick	2/9 Unrecorded Rousay	20	
Jane Craigie	2/12 Unrecorded Rousay	35	
Mary Flett	2/12 Unrecorded Rousay	20	
Janet Flett	2/12 Unrecorded Rousay	20	
Mary Harcus	2/13 Unrecorded Rousay	30	
Mary Flaws	2/21 Unrecorded Rousay	40	
Jane Mainland	Saviskaill Rousay	15	
Barbary Craigie	2/42 Unrecorded Rousay	55	E33
Cecilia Craigie	2/42 Unrecorded Rousay	20	B524
Mary Inkster	2/44 Unrecoreded Rousay	45	
Mary Craigie	Quoyostray Rousay	25	
Margaret Clouston	Tou Rousay	15	
Jane Craigie	2/62 Unrecorded Rousay	45	
Barbary Craigie	2/62 Unrecorded Rousay	40	
Jane Craigie	Innister Rousay	20	
Betsy Harcus	Upper Mounsay Rousay	30	
Ann Marwick	Garmount Rousay	25	
Barbara Craigie	4 Egilsay	30	nee Rendall E48
Mary Alexander	15 Egilsay	30	
Barbara Alexander	15 Egilsay	25	
Catherine Foulis	17 Egilsay	50	
Francis Craigie	17 Egilsay	10	
Eliza Craigie	35 Egilsay	40	
Janet Craigie	35 Egilsay	35	
Euphemia Mowat	Aicres St Andrews	25	
Ellen Spence	Cooperage St Andrews	45	
Margaret Spence	Cooperage St Andrews	30	

Ann Leask	?? Ness St Andrews	30
Margaret Linney	Quies St Andrews	30
Elleanor Eunson	Tuick Ha St Andrews	45
Margaret Reid	Peterhouse St Andrews	25
Margaret Mowat	Upper Messigat St Andrews	15
Margaret Esson	Little Grind St Andrews	65
Isabella Drummond	Little Grind St Andrews	35
Jannet Muir	Little Vattiegal St Andrews	40
Barbara Gorn	Hill Head St Andrews	15
Margaret Laughton	Heatherglen St Andrews	35
Christian Lennie	Windbrek St Andrews	35
Mary Garrioch	Brough St Andrews	30
Mary Wallace	Voy St Andrews	20
Catherine Wallace	Voy St Andrews	20
Isabella Wallace	Voy St Andrews	20
Margaret Bews	Aysick St Andrews	35
Jane Paplay	Newcastle St Andrews	55
Barbara Linnay	Little Derbyshire St Andrews	35
Margaret Linnie	Purtabreak St Andrews	45
Jane Delday	Lochend St Andrews	20
Betsy Delday	Lochend St Andrews	15
Hellen Gaddie	Lochend St Andrews	50
Margaret Voy	Waterslap St Andrews	20
Christian Garrioch	Turnpike St Andrews	45
Barbara Sinclair	Nebester Cross Sanday	45
Betsy Berston	Nebester Cross Sanday	30
Barbara Slatter	Castlegreen Cross Sanday	30
Mary Muir	Brughhill Cross Sanday	35
Jean Brock	Storehouse? Cross Sanday	15 bonnet maker
Isabella Muir	Gateside Houses Burness Sanday	55
Jane Muir	Gateside Houses Burness Sanday	50
Betsy Muir	Gateside Houses Burness Sanday	25
Helen Scott	Rock Houses Burness Sanday	40
Betsy King	Hermisgarth Houses Burness Sanday	30
Christian Drummond	Hermisgarth Houses Burness Sanday	50
Margaret Peace	Skelbrae Town Sanday	35
Jennet Peace	Skelbrae Town Sanday	30
Barbara Peace	Skelbrae Town Sanday	25
Bella Brass	North Dyke Sandwick	25
Mary Moar	Scarwell Sandwick	25
Catherine Harvey	Scarwell Sandwick	20
Margaret Harvey	Scarwell Sandwick	15
Elisa Harvey	Scarwell Sandwick	25
Betty Moar	Scarwell Sandwick	25
Margaret Hackland	Scarwell Sandwick	45
Margaret Garson	Scarwell Sandwick	25
Bella Garson	Scarwell Sandwick	20

Catherine Moar	Scarwell Sandwick	20
Jannet Garson	Housegarth Sandwick	55
Martha Smith	North Unigar Sandwick	20
Barbara Smith	North Unigar Sandwick	20
Marjory Brass	North Unigar Sandwick	45
Margaret Harvey	Linklater Sandwick	20
Catherine Twatt	Linklater Sandwick	30
Mary Kirkness	Linklater Sandwick	20
Catherine Brass	Linklater Sandwick	20
Margaret Brass	Linklater Sandwick	20
Graham Garson	Linklater Sandwick	30
Margaret Johnston	Scaebrae Sandwick	50
Catherine Johnston	Scaebrae Sandwick	25
May Johnston	Scaebrae Sandwick	20
Sarah Johnston	Scaebrae Sandwick	15
Ann Johnston	Scaebrae Sandwick	14
Margaret Garson	Scaebrae Sandwick	25
Margaret Linklater	Scaebrae Sandwick	25
Christina Linklater	Scaebrae Sandwick	20
Margaret Hourston	Hourston Sandwick	15
Catherine Hourston	Hourston Sandwick	35
Ann Hourston	Hourston Sandwick	35
Mary Harvey	Kirkness Sandwick	25
Catherine Hackland	Kirkness Sandwick	20
Euphemia Hackland	Kirkness Sandwick	20
Mary Hackland	Kirkness Sandwick	15
Margaret Hackland	Kirkness Sandwick	14
Janet Twatt	Vetquoy Sandwick	35
Margaret Garson	Vetquoy Sandwick	25
Elspet Garson	Vetquoy Sandwick	35
Janet Garson	Vetquoy Sandwick	25
Catherine Twatt	Brecks of Rango Sandwick	30
Catherine Brass	Brecks of Rango Sandwick	20
Margaret Brass	Brecks of Rango Sandwick	15
Mary Spence	Brecks of Rango Sandwick	15
Elizabeth Peace	West House Sandwick	35
Elizabeth Marwick	Braehead Sandwick	30
Marjory Marwick	Braehead Sandwick	25
Martha Marwick	Braehead Sandwick	20
Elizabeth Linklater	Chamber of Velyan Sandwick	30
Catherin Linklater	Chamber of Velyan Sandwick	25
Margaret Stockan	Nebigar Sandwick	20
Robina Peace	Cupaday Sandwick	20
Janet Brown	Garricot Sandwick	40
Janet Stockan	Chamber Silkin Sandwick	45
Barbra Folster	Oram Unigar Sandwick	40
Catherine Moar	Oram Unigar Sandwick	30

Marjory Brass	Croval Sandwick	55	
Marjory Brass	Croval Sandwick	25	
Jacoba Brass	Croval Sandwick	15	
Jane Brass	Croval Sandwick	15	
Sarah Hay	Rosebank Sandwick	15	
Catherine Louttit	Cot Sandwick	35	
Isabella Flett	Mount Pleasant Sandwick	40	
Margaret Robertson	Mount Pleasant Sandwick	15	
Catherine Rowland	? Sandwick	45	
Betty Rowland	? Sandwick	14	
Elizabeth Hutchison	Guibro Shapinsay	35	straw maker
Mary Sinclair	Cows Shapinsay	30	
Jane Heddle	Furrowend Shapinsay	30	
Isabella Brodie	Brodgear Shapinsay	35	
Jane Linklater	Shoreside Shapinsay	35	
Jane Nicholson	Shoreside Shapinsay	45	
Margaret Nicholson	Shoreside Shapinsay	45	
Margaret Heddle	Shoreside Shapinsay	40	
Margaret Work	? Shapinsay	50	
Barbara Work	Grassquoy Shapinsay	50	
Ann Heddle	Dogpow Shapinsay	55	
Margaret Michall	Niesthouse Shapinsay	50	
Marion Work	New House Shapinsay	60	
Jane Sinclair	Hannataft Shapinsay	30	
Christian Russell	Nether Sty Shapinsay	50	
Mary Heddle	Little Ousquoy Shapinsay	25	
Mary Guthrie	Kirkhall Shapinsay	30	
Janet Hepburn	Kirkhall Shapinsay	30	
Esther Liddle	Linton Shapinsay	45	
Margaret Heddle	Heather House Shapinsay	30	
Elizabeth Heddle	Heather House Shapinsay	40	
Harriet Drummond	Firhall Shapinsay	40	
Janet Merriman	Little Foxton Shapinsay	55	
Mary Merriman	Little Foxton Shapinsay	25	
Margaret Merriman	Little Foxton Shapinsay	30	
Margaret Skethway	Gateside Shapinsay	30	
Isabella Skethway	Gateside Shapinsay	20	
Elizabeth Skethway	Gateside Shapinsay	15	
Mary Work	Newhouse Shapinsay	40	
Sibbyla Gullion	Little Gorn Shapinsay	47	
Margaret Work	Clate Shapinsay	20	
Esther Work	Clate Shapinsay	15	
Mary Ross	St Margarets Hope S Ronaldsay	30	bonnet maker
Mary Russland	Coolack St Peters S Ronaldsay	20	milliner
Jessie Russland	Coolack St Peters S Ronaldsay	15	milliner
Ann Ross	Grimness St Peters S Ronaldsay	35	bonnet maker
Barbara Muir	Sandwick St Marys	70	

Margaret Muir	Sandwick St Marys	30
Margaret Muir	Sandwick St Marys	30
Rachel Thomson	Dam St Marys	20
Janet Johnston	Dam St Marys	40
Margaret Johnston	Dam St Marys	35
Barbara Sinclair	Gaira St Marys	35
Elizabeth Sinclair	Gaira St Marys	20
Helen Sinclair	Gaira St Marys	20
Mary Sinclair	Gaira St Marys	15
Catherine Gutcher	Gaira St Marys	25
Isabella Gutcher	Gaira St Marys	20
Christina Budge	Settigar St Marys	15
Ann Mowat	Settigar St Marys	45
Janet Symeson	Greenvale St Marys	40
Janet Symeson	Greenvale St Marys	14
Ann Symeson	Greenvale St Marys	12
Catherine Dunnet	Nether House St Marys	15
Ellen Taylor	Quoyball St Marys	25
Barbara Tomison	Head St Marys	40
Jane Tomison	Broll St Marys	30
Margaret Annal	Stane St Marys	15
Barbara Wishart	Bow of Linklater St Marys	25
Ann Wishart	Bow of Linklater St Marys	20
Margaret Dunnet	Lyth St Marys	15
Jane Dunnet	Lyth St Marys	30
Ann Dunnet	Lyth St Marys	25
Betsy Dunnet	Lyth St Marys	20
Margaret Sinclair	Windwick St Marys	14
Jean Gunn	Windwick St Marys	20
Grace Velzian	Windwick St Marys	14
Juliana Velzian	Windwick St Marys	12
Mary Tomison	Halcro St Marys	15
Helen Symison	North Flaws St Marys	40
Catherine Duncan	Flaws St Marys	25
Catherine Miller	Flaws St Marys	55
Sibella Miller	Flaws St Marys	15
Catherine Miller	Flaws St Marys	15
Jean Mowat	Quoys of Grindally St Marys	15
Elizabeth McIvor	Dundas Muir St Marys	15
Catherine McIvor	Dundas Muir St Marys	14
Barbara Matches	Ossquoy St Marys	20
Janet Matches	Ossquoy St Marys	14
Peggy Matches	Ossquoy St Marys	12
Annie Thomson	Knowe St Marys	25
Catherine Thomson	Knowe St Marys	14
Margaret Rosie	Holland St Marys	15
Isabella Thomson	Hill St Marys	45

Hellen Duncan	Hill St Marys	35	
Margaret Cruikshank	Quoys St Marys	14	
Margaret Green	Quoys St Marys	15	
Isabella Green	Quoys St Marys	13	
Christian Budge	Grahamston St Marys	15	
Barbara Brown	Vigie St Marys	15	
Margaret Brown	Vigie St Marys	15	
Catherine Rosie	Banks St Marys	20	
Margaret Rosie	Banks St Marys	20	
Mary Aitkin	Lyddal St Marys	14	
Catherine Mowat	Isbister St Marys	15	
Margaret Mowat	Isbister St Marys	15	
Margaret Thomson	Clett St Marys	25	
Jean Flaws	Clett St Marys	30	
Christian Flaws	Clett St Marys	25	
Stewartina Cursator	Clett St Marys	20	
Catherine Cursator	Clett St Marys	20	
Margaret Cursator	Clett St Marys	15	
Jane Rosie	Ballgreen St Marys	45	
Isabella Rosie	Ballgreen St Marys	15	
Margaret Rosie	Ballgreen St Marys	13	
Jane Cursator	Burrowstown St Marys	14	
Jean Gutcher	Gunnerhill St Marys	20	
Janet Gutcher	Gunnerhill St Marys	20	
Margaret Gutcher	Gunnerhill St Marys	16	
Jemima Harper	Outertown Stromness	15	
Catherine Flett	Outertown Stromness	15	
Jane Irvine	Outertown Stromness	40	
Helen Flett	Outertown Stromness	35	
Margaret Moar	Innertown Stromness	55	
Catherine Card	Innertown Stromness	40	
Wilhemina Brass	Innertown Stromness	12	
Helen Flett	Innertown Stromness	35	
Ann Brown	Innertown Stromness	20	
Barbara Brown	Innertown Stromness	15	
Catherine Byas	Innertown Stromness	12	
Janet Linklater	Innertown Stromness	40	
Sibella Leith	Cairston Stromness	35	
Margaret Spence	Cairston Stromness	35	
Margaret Knarston	Cairston Stromness	15	
Margery Robertson	Cairston Stromness	40	
Margaret Irvine	Cairston Stromness	25	
Christina Croy	Cairston Stromness	35	
Isabella Croy	Cairston Stromness	15	
Bettsy Flett	Quholm Stromness	35	strawknitter
Isabella Irvine	Quholm Stromness	25	strawknitter
Isabella Irvine	Quholm Stromness	25	strawknitter

Jannet Irvine	Quholm Stromness	20	strawknitter
Shusan Irvine	Quholm Stromness	15	strawknitter
Helen Linklater	Quholm Stromness	30	strawknitter
Ann Hourston	Quholm Stromness	15	strawknitter
Margaret Hourston	Quholm Stromness	15	strawknitter
Margaret Linklater	Quholm Stromness	50	strawknitter
Jean Isbister	Quholm Stromness	30	strawknitter
Christian Dikson	Quholm Stromness	35	strawknitter
Mariah Scott	Quholm Stromness		strawknotter
Isabella Baikie	Quholm Stromness	30	strawknotter
Catherine Towers	Quholm Stromness	35	strawknotter
Margaret Towers	Quholm Stromness	30	strawknotter
Ann Towers	Quholm Stromness	25	strawknotter
Isabella Marwick	Quholm Stromness	30	strawknotter
Margaret Rouland	Quholm Stromness	25	strawknotter
Marjary Corrigal	Redland Stromness	40	strawknitter
Marjarey Norn	Redland Stromness	25	strawknitter
Jannet Norn	Redland Stromness	20	strawknitter
Catherine Clouston	Redland Stromness	15	strawknotter
Margaret Linklater	Kirbister Stromness	15	
Jannet Linklater	Kirbister Stromness	13	
Catherine Wilson	Kirbister Stromness	30	
Margaret Wilson	Kirbister Stromness	10	
Margaret Hunter	Kirbister Stromness	45	
Ann Hunter	Kirbister Stromness	25	
Elizabeth Hunter	Kirbister Stromness	30	
Isabella Hunter	Kirbister Stromness	20	
Margery Louttit	Kirbister Stromness	55	
Mary Ann Robb	Ness Stromness	30	
Jean Moar	South End Stromness	50	
Isabella Irvine	South End Stromness	55	
Jean Baikie	South End Stromness	35	
Catherine Baikie	South End Stromness	25	
Hannah Anderson	South End Stromness	55	
Eliza B N Miller	South End Stromness	20	
May Sabeston	Knockhall Stromness	20	
Catherine Linklater	Citadel Stromness	20	
Janet Linklater	Citadel Stromness	20	
Ann Taylor	Main St Stromness	15	
Clementina Malish	Main St Stromness	55	
Betsy Allan	Main St Stromness	15	
Margaret Mowat	Main St Stromness	30	
Jane Flett	Main St Stromness	25	
Margery Sinclair	Main St Stromness	65	
Margaret Baikie	Main St Stromness	35	
Isabella Clouston	Main St Stromness	50	
Marjory Garriock	Main St Stromness	45	

Catharine Lion	Main St Stromness	45	
Janet Brown	Main St Stromness	25	
Margaret Scott	Main St Stromness	30	
Betsy Taylor	Main St Stromness	14	
Ann Wards	Main St Stromness	40	
Margaret White	Main St Stromness	55	
Cecilia Brock	Main St Stromness	20	
Ann Craigie	Main St Stromness	20	bonnet maker
Eliza Muir	Main St Stromness	30	
Margaret Folster	Main St Stromness	25	bonnet maker
Jean Scott	Main St Stromness	25	
Margaret Wards	Main St Stromness	20	
Margaret Miller	Main St Stromness	25	bonnet maker
Charlotte Mowat	Main St Stromness	35	
Margaret Velzian	Main St Stromness	30	
Christiana Hackland	Main St Stromness	15	
Ann Wilson	Main St Stromness	55	
Christiana Young	Main St Stromness	20	
Margaret Sinclair	Main St Stromness	50	
Jean Rich	Main St Stromness	45	
Margaret Shearer	Main St Stromness	40	
Jean Young	Main St Stromness	20	
Margaret Linklater	Main St Stromness	35	
Isabella Robertson	Main St Stromness	30	
Jemima Robertson	Main St Stromness	8	
May Sabiston	Main St Stromness	25	
Helen Sabiston	Main St Stromness	20	
Mary Moar	Main St Stromness	30	
Margaret Thomson	Main St Stromness	45	
Betsy Brown	Main St Stromness	35	
Betsy Brown	Main St Stromness	15	
Ann Inkster	Main St Stromness	45	
Catherine Inkster	Main St Stromness	15	
Ann Tait	Main St Stromness	30	
Betsy Hacklan	Main St Stromness	25	
Margaret Hacklan	Main St Stromness	20	
Jean Esson	Main St Stromness	30	
Barbara Thomson	Main St Stromness	25	
Jean Fiddler	Main St Stromness	35	
Elizabeth Tait	Main St Stromness	45	
Susan Snody	Main St Stromness	35	
Catherine Break	Main St Stromness	35	
Margaret Mowat	Main St Stromness	30	
Margaret Robertson	Main St Stromness	50	
Charlotte Robertson	Main St Stromness	25	foreign born
Barbara Davidson	Main St Stromness	60	
Isabella Tait	Main St Stromness	30	straw hat maker

Mary Tait	Main St Stromness	35	
Mary Tait	Main St Stromness	10	
Ann Esson	Main St Stromness	40	
Betsy Johnston	Main St Stromness	35	
Barbara Lion	Main St Stromness	50	
Margaret Lion	Main St Stromness	15	
William Heddle	Main St Stromness	50	straw manufacturer
Jean Mecay	Main St Stromness	30	
Jemima Jack	Main St Stromness	10	
Isabella Brown	Main St Stromness	45	
Moly Louttit	Grays Buildings Stromness	60	
Margaret Louttit	Grays Buildings Stromness	35	
Mary Louttit	Grays Buildings Stromness	15	
Helen Borwick	Grays Buildings Stromness	25	
Margaret Louttit	Grays Buildings Stromness	15	
Christian Louttit	Grays Buildings Stromness	55	
Hanna Louttit	Grays Buildings Stromness	20	
Janet Setter	Grays Buildings Stromness	50	
Ann Thomson	Grays Buildings Stromness	40	
Ann Norn	Grays Buildings Stromness	25	
Hanna Corrigal	Grays Buildings Stromness	30	
Janet Mouat	Grays Buildings Stromness	60	
Euphemia Gray	Grays Buildings Stromness	20	
Isabella Clouston	Grays Buildings Stromness	25	
Charlot Leask	Grays Buildings Stromness	20	
Mary Garroch	Grays Buildings Stromness	20	straw bonnet maker
Ann Spence	Grays Buildings Stromness	25	
Ann Linklater	Grays Buildings Stromness	40	
Sally Linklater	Grays Buildings Stromness	30	
Ann Allan	Grays Buildings Stromness	30	
Cathrine Rendall	Grays Buildings Stromness	30	
Jane Ballanden	Grays Buildings Stromness	45	
Jane Ballanden	Grays Buildings Stromness	20	
Elizabeth Ballanden	Grays Buildings Stromness	15?	
Barbra Reid	Grays Buildings Stromness	35	
Cathrine Betton	Grays Buildings Stromness	35	
Jane Thomison	Grays Buildings Stromness	45	
Margaret Thomison	Grays Buildings Stromness	10	
Betsy Spence	Grays Buildings Stromness	45	
Ann Spence	Grays Buildings Stromness	15	
Isabella Hackland	Grays Buildings Stromness	40	
Margery Hackland	Grays Buildings Stromness	35	
Cathrine McKay	Grays Buildings Stromness	60	
Elizabeth McKay	Grays Buildings Stromness	20	
Jessy Maxwell	Grays Buildings Stromness	25	
Margaret Corrigall	Grays Buildings Stromness	20	
Ann Corrigall	Grays Buildings Stromness	10	

Marget Smith	Grays Buildings Stromness	40	
Cicla Sutherland	Grays Buildings Stromness	35	straw manufacturer
Janet Steward	Grays Buildings Stromness	60	
Margaret Steward	Grays Buildings Stromness	20	
Helen Steward	Grays Buildings Stromness	15	
Janet Steward	Grays Buildings Stromness	20	
Christiana Corrigal	Grays Buildings Stromness	50	
Margaret Corrigal	Grays Buildings Stromness	20	
Christiana Corrigal	Grays Buildings Stromness	15	
Peterina Corrigal	Grays Buildings Stromness	12	
Mary Nurquoy	Grays Buildings Stromness	30	
Elizabeth Leask	Main St Stromness	40	
Catherine Louttit	Main St Stromness	25	straw sorter ?
Robert Clouston	Main St Stromness	55	straw manufacturer
Margaret Flett	Stromness	25	
Margaret Irvine	Stromness	25	
Margaret Archibald	Stromness	20	
Marion Sinclair	Stromness	30	
Jean Oman	Stromness	45	
Jean Oman	Stromness	20	
Betsy Isbsiter	Stromness	30	
Helen Robertson	Stromness	30	
Mary Leith	Stromness	40	
Gersey Firth	Stromness	60	
Janet Louttit	Stromness	40	
Margaret Creelman	Stromness	25	
Mary Creelman	Stromness	25	straw bonnet maker
Mary McDonald	Stromness	40	
Janet Creelman	Stromness	15	
Betsy Gray	Stromness	20	
Bell Brodie	Stromness	60	
Elizabeth Bews?	Stromness	25	
Helen Bews?	Stromness	20	
Christiana Mainland	Stromness	70	
Christiana Mainland	Stromness	30	
Barbara Mainland	Stromness	30	
Margaret Craigie	Stromness	40	
Margaret Craigie	Stromness	15	
Ann Craigie	Stromness	6	
Ann Beatton	Stromness	40	
Mary Oman	Stromness	35	
Isabella Mowat	Stromness	30	
Christiana Johnston	Stromness	20	
James Corrigall	Stromness	30	merchant & straw agent
Mary Oman	Stromness	30	
Ann Harvey	Stromness	40	
Jean Fosby	Stromness	14	

Margaret Dishan	Stromness	15	
Ann Dishan	Stromness	10	
William Dishan (M)	Stromness	7	
Margaret Hackland	Stromness	40	
William Clouston	Stromness	30	straw maker
Wilhemina Smith	Stromness	35	straw bonnet maker
Marjory Muir	Stromness	20	
Janet Downie	Stromness	45	
Catharine Moar	Stromness	35	
Margaret Leask	Stromness	45	
Mary Mowat	Stromness	15	
Ann Louttit	Stromness	25	
Jane Mowat	Stromness	30	
Janet Mowat	Stromness	11	
Ann Dunnet	Stromness	25	
Barbara Mowat	Stromness	25	
Janet Mowat	Stromness	40	
Ann Mowat	Stromness	35	
Elizabeth Clouston	Stromness	55	
Betsy Linklater	Stromness	20	
Catherine Inksetter	Stromness	30	
Hellen Robertson	Stromness	50	
Hellen Towers	North End Stromness	25	
Janet Towers	North End Stromness	20	
Ann Towers	North End Stromness	15	
Susanna Thompson	North End Stromness	25	
Euphemia Corrigall	North End Stromness	20	
Elizabeth Mowat	North End Stromness	35	
Elizabeth Sinclair	North End Stromness	40	
Catherine Harvey	North End Stromness	30	
Christian Johnston	North End Stromness	30	
Margaret Brass	North End Stromness	30	
Cicillia Louttit	North End Stromness	45	
Graham Corrigall (F)	North End Stromness	50	
Mary Leask	North End Stromness	25	
Isabella Leask	North End Stromness	25	
Ann Leask	North End Stromness	20	
Janet Knarston	North End Stromness	40	
Catherine Stanger	North End Stromness	45	
Mary Mowat	North End Stromness	40	
Euphemia Rowland	North End Stromness	25	
Gordon Flett (F)	North End Stromness	55	bonnet maker
Ann Flett	North End Stromness	20	
Janet Flett	North End Stromness	14	
May Laughton	North End Stromness	60	
May Laughton	North End Stromness	35	
Elizabeth Flett	North End Stromness	20	

Margaret Twat	North End Stromness	30	
Isabella Flett	North End Stromness	25	
Jane Morwick	North End Stromness	30	
Margaret Clouston	North End Stromness	40	
John Flett	North End Stromness	55	straw manufacturer
Janet Sabiston?	North End Stromness	45	
Cathrine Sabiston?	North End Stromness	15	
Elizabeth Sabiston?	North End Stromness	10	
Isabella Tait	North End Stromness	45	
Margaret Linklater	North End Stromness	30	
Catherine Louttit	North End Stromness	50	
Isabella Smith	North End Stromness	40	
Jane Norn	North End Stromness	35	
Jane Norn	North End Stromness	12	
Margaret Norn	North End Stromness	10	
Catharine Brass	North End Stromness	35	
Margaret Brass	North End Stromness	12	
Catherine Brass	North End Stromness	10	
Catherine Spence	North End Stromness	35	
Elizabeth Spence	North End Stromness	40	
Catherine Spence	North End Stromness	15	
Margaret Spence	North End Stromness	14	
Betsey Spence	North End Stromness	8	
Christina Rowland	North End Stromness	50	
Catherine Baikie	Queen St Stromness	50	
Catherine Mowat	Queen St Stromness	55	
Elizabeth Spence	Queen St Stromness	40	
Ann Spence	Queen St Stromness	8	
Elizabeth Spence	Queen St Stromness	6	
Christian Ballenden	Queen St Stromness	45	
Ann Spence	Queen St Stromness	60	
Catherine Tait	Queen St Stromness	30	
Catherine Tait	Queen St Stromness	15	
Jane Tait	Queen St Stromness	15	
Isabella Tait	Queen St Stromness	6	
Margaret Inkster	Queen St Stromness	70	
Helen Hunter	Queen St Stromness	40	
Helen Hunter	Queen St Stromness	9	
Eliza Annal	Queen St Stromness	30	
Charlot Scarth	Queen St Stromness	55	
Mary Anderson	Queen St Stromness	25	
Janet Harvey	Queen St Stromness	45	
Helen Harvey	Queen St Stromness	40	
Sabelia Flett	Queen St Stromness	25	
Janet Murray	Queen St Stromness	25	
Margaret Murray	Queen St Stromness	20	
Isabella Murray	Queen St Stromness	25	

Jane Linklater	Queen St Stromness	30	
Janet Linklater	Queen St Stromness	13	
Elizabeth Adamson	Queen St Stromness	45	
Margaret Moar	Queen St Stromness	35	
Ann Baikie	Queen St Stromness	45	
Ann Baikie	Queen St Stromness	20	
Christina Baikie	Queen St Stromness	15	
Euphemia Baikie	Queen St Stromness	10	
Catherine Sabiston?	Queen St Stromness	60	
Catherine Sabiston?	Queen St Stromness	30	
Mary Sabiston?	Queen St Stromness	20	
Elizabeth Sabiston?	Queen St Stromness	15	
Barbara Miller	Rothiesholm Lady Kirk Stronsay	40	
Mary Taylor	Downatown Lady Kirk Stronsay	40	
Mary Chalmers	Dirdal Lady Kirk Stronsay	25	straw hat maker
Barbara Elphinstone	Bombasting Lady Kirk Stronsay	45	
Barbara Scott	Lochend Lady Kirk Stronsay	50	
Cathrine Devine	Clyth Lady Kirk Stronsay	65	
Ann Thompson	Grindally St Peters Stronsay	35	
Barbara Scott	Warthill/Wardhill St Peters Stronsay	20	
Elizabeth Chalmers	Midgarth St Peters Stronsay	40	
Margaret Sinclair	Lower Midgarth St Peters Stronsay	30	
Margaret Miller	Hilly House St Peters Stronsay	15	
Anne Cooper	Hilly House St Peters Stronsay	15	
Anne Cooper	Whitehall Village Stronsay	15	
Barbara Sinclair	Whitehall Village Stronsay	15	
Christy Mudie	Holland St Nicholas Stronsay	35	
Jean Reid	Southquoy St Nicholas Stronsay	55	
Margaret Reid	Southquoy St Nicholas Stronsay	45	
Susan Wilson	Wing, Walls	25	bonnet maker
Elisabeth Seater	Pierowall Westray	15	
May Balfour	Gateside Westray	45	
Jean Reid	Cage Westray	15	
Margaret Reid	Cage Westray	20	
Barbara Mason	Brugh Westray	35	
Isabella Grey	Brugh Westray	55	
Betty Line	Nistegar Westray	45	
Mary Paplie	Dogtua Westray	40	

1851 Census Records of Strawplaiters

Name	Address	Age	Status	Notes
Catherine Flett	Moan, Firth	45	single	
Catherine Jack	Horraldshay Firth	69	single	
Sebla Flett	Society School Firth visitor	34	single	visitor
Catherine Corrigall	Snabba Firth	50	single	
Cicilia Firth	Thickbigging Firth	40	single	
Cicilia Wilson	Thickbigging Firth	46	single	
Margaret Yorston	Breckan Firth	50	single	
Mary Corrigall	South House Redland Firth	54	single	
Christiana Hurrie	Nistabin Outhouse Firth	45	single	
Jane Sletter	Little Lettily	58	single	
Jane Knarston	?Stenness	61	single	pauper
Margaret Leask	Waterskap Stenness	54	single	pauper
Betsy Johnson	Upper Gear Stenness	33	widow	
Betsy Buchan	Breckan Stenness	52	single	
Margaret Louttit	Lower Gear Stenness	33	single	
Christina Louttit	Lower Gear Stenness	31	single	
Christina Baikie	Loan Stenness	44	single	
Mary Corrigall	Maco? Stenness	30	single	visitor
Betsty Leask	?Stenness	67	single	
Euphina Leask	?Stenness	64	single	
Margaret Leask	?Stenness	50	single	
Sarah Leask	?Stenness	47	single	
Betsty Flett	Stoureisdale Stenness	45	single	
Mary Bews	Nether Bigswale Stenness	26	single	
Anne Gray	Bigswale Stenness	53	single	
Anne Gray	Bigswale Stenness	18	single	cousin
Margaret Isbister	Breck Stenness	25	single	
Mary Goudie	Sherounda Stenness	19	single	straw bonnet maker
Catherine Hourston	Hozen Harray	30	single	
Mary Hourston	Hozen Harray	28	single	
Jessy King	Dilly Harray	38	single	
Mary Hourston	Brake on Commonty Harray	25	single	
Jean Linklater	Brake on Commonty Harray	50	single	formerly strawplaiter
Susan Clouston	Brake on Commonty Harray	29	single	lame straw bonnet plaiter
Elizabeth Linklater	Holodyke Harray	24	single	
Jean Hay	Upper Mithouse Harray	25	single	
Peggy Stanger	Upper Mithouse Harray	65	single	pauper former strawplaiter
Margaret Smith	Nisthouse Harray	39	single	former straw hat maker

Name	Place	Age/Status
Margaret Holland	Brake on Commonty Harray	42 married
Elizabeth Marwick	Upper Bigging Harray	55 married
Marjery Harper	Upper Bigging Harray	66 single
Christian Flett	Lammaquoy Harray	67 single straw bonnet maker
Jean Manson	Stripol Harray	26 single
Margaret Manson	Stripol Harray	44 widow
Elizabeth Manson	Stripol Harray	43 single
Helen Manson	Stripol Harray	33 married
Marian Flett	Gossapin Harray	27 single
Hellen Flett	Gossapin Harray	24 single
Isabella Johnston	Quina Harray	42 single
Ann Firth	Tiveth Harray	49 single
Isabella Smith	Tiveth Harray	24 single
Mary Sinclair	Overakelda Harray	40 single
Helen Borwick	Nisthouse Harray	33 single
Mary Sinclair	Beboran Harray	22 single
Betsy Scott	Queena Harray	45 single
Jean Scott	Queena Harray	35 single
Catherine Robertson	Moan Harray	40 single stocking knitter
Margaret Robertson	Biggins Harray	42 single
Margaret Hourston	Twargan Harray	22 single
Betsy Hourston	Twargan Harray	19 single
Mary Velzian	Appihouse Harray	23 single
Christina Anderson	Chamber Appihouse Harray	39 single?
Isabela Clouston	Boardhouse Harray	27 single
Margaret Louttit	Overhouse Harray	18 single
Hellen Louttit	Overhouse Harray	20 single
Marjory Brown	Queer Harray	56 single
Christina Brown	Queer Harray	50 single
Margaret Brown	Queer Harray	45 single
Isabella Flett	Chamber of Garth Harray	40 married
Mary Leask	Bow Harray	50 single?
Mary Corrigall	Suraquoy Harray	25 single
May Kirkness	Nairhouse Harray	52 single
Betsy Flett	Vola Harray	25 single agricultural labourer
Mary Isbister	Heybreck Harray	32 single
Ann Corrigall	North House Harray	25 single
Christina Scott	Fursbreck Harray	57 single
Ann Burges	Roadside Eday	50 single
Christian Flett	Midhouse Evie	45 single?
Ann Baikie	St Andrews Evie	26 single
Euphemia Corrigal	Upper Pow Evie	69 widow
Jane Baikie	Upper Pow Evie	23 single
Janet Flett	Newhall Evie	40 single
Charlotte Miller	Hewin Evie	18 married ? formerly strawplaiter

Mary Hutchison	Clickamin Evie	20 single
Christian Thomson	Castlehill Evie	40 married
Jessie Hourston	Mount Vita Evie	48 single harvest labourer
Ann Hourston	Mount Vita Evie	28 single harvest labourer
Ann Hourston	Mount Vita Evie	22 single ? harvest labourer
Ann Calder	Turndale Evie	19 single
Phebe Calder	Turndale Evie	26 single
Betsy Calder	Turndale Evie	15 single
Mary Corrigall	Neigarth Evie	29 single
Betsy Corrigall	Neigarth Evie	22 single
Ann Corrigall	Neigarth Evie	19 single
Magadaline Sabiston	Grena Evie	16 single
Martha Leask	Quoys Evie	33 single
Magadaline Leask	Quoys Evie	25 single
Mary Leask	Quoys Evie	19 single
Jane Corrigall	Rushabrek Evie	22 single
Christian Turnbull	Dyke Evie	70 widow pauper former strawplaiter
Jane Hourston	Boggie Evie	23 single
Martha Hourston	Boggie Evie	18 single
Ann Anderson	Indnagar Evie	16 single
Margaret Anderson	Indnagar Evie	41 single
Jacobina Anderson	Indnagar Evie	35 married croft 3 acre
Margaret Ballendine	Mystray Evie	27 single
Mary Irvine	Persecution Evie	25 single
Betty Irvine	Persecution Evie	22 single
Barbara Mainland	…Insby Evie	38 single visitor
Ann Louttit	North…Rendall	30 single
Margaret Sclater	…breck Rendall	38 single agricultural labourer
Jessy Euson	Slinghorn? Rendall	17 single
Crawford Murray	Newhouse Rendall	31 single
Barbara Borwick	Su…lay Rendall	41 single
Ann Wood	…igar Rendall	23 single
Ellen Dishan	Betho Rendall	22 single
Catherine Esson	Little Lyking Rendall	33 single
Mary Dreaver	Little Skiddow Rendall	40 single
Barbara Bichan	Clibberbreck Rendall	43 single visitor
Maryann Hurie	Hallbreck Rendall	35 widow nee Moar
Janet Gaudie	Netherskaill Birsay	49 widow
Dinah Spence	House Birsay	65 single
Ann Taylor	Little Comlaquoy Birsay	30 married
Margat Taylor	Little Gridgar Birsay	15 single
Helen Johnston	Little Waird Birsay	20 single
Elizabeth Marwick	Little Waird Birsay	74 widow
Elizabeth Taylor	Park of Windbreck Birsay	46 single
Margaret Taylor	Park of Windbreck Birsay	36 single
Hannah Philip	On the Hill Birsay	46 single

147

Margaret Stickler	Cote Liaquoy Birsay	19 single
Mary Mowat	Roebreck Birsay	40 single
Margaret Mowat	Roebreck Birsay	38 single
Ann Stickler	Stara Birsay	18 single
Margaret Moar	Stara Birsay	47 single
Catherine Moar	Stara Birsay	21 single
Mary Moar	Stara Birsay	15 single
Catherine Johnston	Leary Birsay	31 single
Jean Burwick	Quoylonga Birsay	17 single
Margaret Burwick	Quoylonga Birsay	16 single
Margaret Philip	Dales Birsay	26 single
Catherine Hunter	Scorn Birsay	39 single
Marion Hunter	Scorn Birsay	35 single
Catherine Hunter	Scorn 2 Birsay	38 single
Janet Houry	New Howland Birsay	44 widow
Catherine Baikie	Nisthouse Birsay	26 single
Betty Baikie	Nisthouse Birsay	21 single
Mary Baikie	Nisthouse Birsay	17 single
Ann Breck	Gairsty Birsay	37 single
Mary Meadows	Geyron Birsay	18 single
Ann Taylor	Turmiston Birsay	22 single
Margaret Taylor	at Turmiston Birsay	26 single
Margaret Linklater	Loughend Birsay	63 single
Margaret Mowat	Biggin Birsay	50 single aunt
Margaret Mowat	Biggin Birsay	25 single niece
Elizabeth Stanger	Runa Birsay	19 single
Margaret Moar	Spurdagrove Birsay	39 married
Cathring Ritch	Festerger Birsay	42 single
Mary Ritch	Festerger Birsay	38 single
Margaret Kirkness	Claybraes Birsay	19 single
Ann Moar	Skedge Birsay	32 single
Jane Moar	Lea Birsay	16 single
Margaret Moar	Lea Birsay	15 single
Margaret Folster	Howquoy Birsay	25 single married 1863 ?
Marion Folster	Howquoy Birsay	16 single
Catherine Folster	Howquoy Birsay	14 single
Maryann Brown	Breck by South Birsay	21 single
Jane Brown	Breck by South Birsay	45 single
Ann Taylor	Glower Birsay	30 single
Mary Stenger	Glower Birsay	26 single
Ann Brown	Ness Birsay	22 single
Ann Mowat	Breck Birsay	59 single b. Rousay
Catherine Hunter	Walkerhouse Birsay	46 single
Ann Hunter	Walkerhouse Birsay	38 single
Mary Adamson	Walkerhouse Birsay	54 single
Marion Adamson	Walkerhouse Birsay	50 single
Mary Linklater	New Birsay	24 single

Margaret Linklater	New Birsay	20 single
Anne McDonald	New Birsay	45 widow
Anne McDonald	New Birsay	12 single
Anne Moar	Old Manse Birsay	43 widow
Mary Comloquoy	Upper Palace Birsay	57 widow
Elizabeth Hunter	Upper Palace Birsay	17 single
Janet Harvey	Place Birsay	25 single
Anne Louttit	Place Birsay	48 single
Margaret Louttit	Place Birsay	56 single
Mary Spence	Place Birsay	18 single
Anne Spence	Place Birsay	16 single
Margaret Spence	Brom Birsay	44 single
Jannet Slatter	On the Commons Birsay	25 single
Margaret Slatter	On the Commons Birsay	23 single
Mary Slatter	On the Commons Birsay	19 single
Barbra Spence	Outside Birsay	18 single
Margaret Harvey	Crogo Birsay	40 single
Catherin Harvey	Crogo Birsay	28 married
Margaret Linklater	Greenhill Birsay	40 single
Jannet Johnston	Purgatory Birsay	14 single
Mary Whittla	Musacalda Birsay	57 single
Marion Whittla	Musacalda Birsay	51 single
Isabella Stanger	Musacalda Birsay	39 single
Ann Johnston	Glebe Birsay	37 single
Jannet Folster	Chinglough Birsay	13 single
Margaret Johnston	Geatnap Birsay	30 single
Catherine Johnston	Geatnap Birsay	22 single
Mary Johnston	Bakith Birsay	25 single
Jane Hunter	Nearhouse Birsay	54 married
Ann Johnston	Nearhouse Birsay	17 single
Mary Taylor	Hawn Birsay	34 single
Margaret Folster	Couperhouse Birsay	47 single
Margaret Johnston	Geatnip Birsay	46 married
Grasel Taylor	Geatnip Birsay	48 married
Margaret Folster	Geatnip Birsay	52 single
Margaret Harvey	Bowan Birsay	20 single
Margaret Bias	Bowan Birsay	30 single
Margaret Stanger	Bowan Birsay	32 single straw bonnet maker
Jannet Stanger	Bowan Birsay	25 single
Mary Whittla	Geseter Birsay	32 single
Bruce Whittla	Geseter Birsay	24 single
Jean Whittla	Geseter Birsay	34 married
Isabella Hunter	Geseter Birsay	16 single
Ann Langskel	Squatter Birsay	32 single
Marey Langskel	Squatter Birsay	23 single
Jean Stanger	Quoir of Hill Birsay	17 single
Margaret Stanger	Quoir of Hill Birsay	13 single

Isabella Stanger	Quoir of Hill Birsay	37	single
Ann Johnston	Fusper Squatter Birsay	28	married
Jean Moar	Fusper Squatter Birsay	39	single
Margaret Langskell	Jubadee Birsay	36	married
Catherin Sinclair	Fusperside Squatter Birsay	48	married
Catherin Moar	Fusperside Squatter Birsay	56	widow
Mary Hunter	Fusperside Squatter Birsay	64	single
Jean Hunter	Fusperside Squatter Birsay	19	single
Isabella Harper	Fuspar Nuan Birsay	46	single
Marey Harper	Fuspar Nuan Birsay	14	single
Jessie Harper	Fuspar Nuan Birsay	11	single
Mary Hunter	Fuspar Squatter Birsay	17	single
Marey Gorie	Fuspar Squatter Birsay	16	single
Margaret Sinclair	Fuspar Squatter Birsay	41	single
Catherine Johnston	Fuspar Squatter Birsay	33	single
Margrat Johnston	Fuspar Squatter Birsay	28	single
Margrat Linklater	Fuspar Squatter Birsay	16	single
May Linklater	Fuspar Squatter Birsay	13	single
Charlot Gorie	Fuspar Squatter Birsay	15	single
Isabella Taylor	Fuspar Waterhouse Birsay	13	single
Cathrine Folster	Fuspar Miran Birsay	37	single
Ann Johnston	Fuspar Squatter Birsay	31	married
Eliza Bias	Fuspar Dond Birsay	37	single
Ann Harvey	Fuspar Wattle Birsay	15	single
Catherine Moar	Slinghorn Birsay	14	single
Jannet Spence	Breckan Birsay	50	single
Ann Spence	Breckan Birsay	30	single
Mary Spence	Windbreck Birsay	56	single
Elizabeth Johnston	New Weskra Birsay	39	single
Martha Johnston	New Weskra Birsay	24	single
Margaret Johnston	New Weskra Birsay	22	single
Ann Johnston	Ranglehall Birsay	36	single
Ann Mowat	Claverhouse Birsay	27	single
Mary Mowat	Little Fea Birsay	26	single
Margaret Spence	Millhouse Birsay	22	single
Catherine Mowat	Deal Birsay	14	single
Ann Spence	Brekiehall Birsay	51	single pauper
Ellen Spence	Millhouse Birsay	22	single
Mary Spence	Millhouse Birsay	20	single
Jannet Spence	Commerical Inn Birsay	34	single
Margaret Spence	Commerical Inn Birsay	23	single
Ann Johnston	Over Hundland Birsay	36	single
Catherine Johnston	Over Hundland Birsay	29	single
Margaret Harvey	Brownbrae Birsay	22	single
Ann Harvey	Brownbrae Birsay	16	single
Ann Sabiston	Upper Skesquoy Birsay	23	single
Mary Spence	Over Hundland Birsay	22	single

Ann Spence	Over Hundland Birsay	19 single
Janet Harvey	Tevah Birsay	25 single
Mady Spence	Relief Birsay	32 widow
Jean Spence	Airie Birsay	16 single
Catherine Harvey	Upper Bigging Birsay	33 married
Margaret Spence	Braehead Birsay	65 married
Maria Johnston	Bigging Birsay	30 single
Mary Johnston	Bigging Birsay	29 single
Margaret Swordie	Dykesdie Birsay	27 single
Ann Swordie	Dykesdie Birsay	25 single
Mary Mode	Water Low Birsay	31 single
Jannet Spence	Breakness Birsay	34 single
Mary Linklater	Mossater Birsay	17 single
Robina Inksetter	Finno Rousay	28 single
Christie Inksetter	Finno Rousay	26 single pauper former strawplaiter
May Turnbull	Oldman Rousay	36 single b. Kirkwall
Ann Yorston	Bare Braes Rousay	27 single
Barbara Craigie	Quoy Faris Rousay	45 single
Margaret Marwick	Hullion Rousay	29 widow nee Craigie straw hat maker
Isabella Johnston	Whitlet Egilsay	17 single
Douglas Yorston	Whistlebear Egilsay	19 single
Isabella Bews	Midskaill Egilsay	28 married
Barbara Craigie	Muklipiece Egilsay	25 single
Barbara Alexander	Nether Skaill Egilsay	38 single
Frances Craigie	Nether Skaill Egilsay	20 single
Catherine Fowlis	Nether Skaill Egilsay	60 single pauper former strawplaiter
Isabella Craigie	South Tofts Egilsay	26 single
Janet Craigie	Howan Egilsay	45 single
Margaret Petrie	Cryon Orphir	15 single
Janet Sletter	Chamber, Quoyangry Orphir	38 single
Christian Sletter	Chamber Quoyangry Orphir	36 single
Jessie Sinclair	Blinks Orphir	27 single
Susan Sinclair	Blinks Orphir	18 single
Celia Thomson	Feea Orphir	62 single pauper former strawplaiter b. Graemsay
Jane Inkster	Grindlay Orphir	21 single
Jessie Inkster	Grindlay Orphir	19 single
Jane Inkster	Grindlay Orphir	17 single
Ann Groundwater	Mounthully Orphir	55 single
Mary Leask	Park Orphir	23 single
Hannah Leask	Park Orphir	15 single
Jane Taylor	Skegbister Orphir	30 single
Margaret Hay	Hill Brae Orphir	29 single
Margaret Farquhar	Chamber Orphir	45 single

151

Christian Ballantine	Bare Brecks Orphir	44 single
Ann Tait	Hannabell Orphir	26 single
Margaret Gunn	Ditch Orphir	27 single b. St Andrews
Helen Inkster	South Side Bourn Orphir	40 single
Margaret Slater	South Side Bourn Orphir	36 single
Margaret Wishart	West Quoy Orphir	40 single
Christian Corner	Aikiley Orphir	37 single
Jean Omand	West Shore Deerness	39 single farm work
Euphemia Matches	Pictil Deerness	42 single farm work
Barbara Linklater	Crabhall Deerness	50 widow knitting
Ann Mowat	Cillerdyke Deerness	45 single pauper
Helen Inkster	Smiddybank Deerness	31 single seamstress
Elizabeth Aitken	Pickletillium Deerness	48 single
Margaret Miller	Trotties Deerness	27 single seamstress
Mary Tait	Little Oback Deerness	26 single 3 children?
Fanny McLeod	Knowes Deerness	45 widow 3 children
Ann Cormack	Little Newark Deerness	54 single
Sarah Foulis	Nutland Deerness	49 single farm work
Anne Stove	North Windbreck Deerness	51 single knitting
Janet Smith	Watermoss Deerness	26 single
Elizabeth Vedder	Little Duncans Deerness	29 single
Margaret Harcus	Scamy Deerness	48 single
Jane Paplay	Cruidy Deerness	34 single
May Stove	Lighthouse Deerness	16 single
Isabella Stove	Lighthouse Deerness	44 single
Margaret Irvine	Cupady Deerness	52 single Copinsay?
Catherine Allan	East Claybrake Holm	48 single
Barbara Dishon	Windwall Holm	27 single
Jane Crear	Loughend Holm	41 single
Ann Petrie	Cot of Braehead Holm	56 single
Jean Sinclair	Cot of Brekquoy Holm	58 single
Janet Maxwell	Cot of Flaws Holm	41 single
Barbara Ritch	Nether Corrigall Graemsay	33 widow b. Rackwick Hoy
Elizabeth Omand	Broad Hill Graemsay	27 single
Margaret Yorston	Loan Lay? Graemsay	50 widow b. Orphir
Margaret Spence	Windbrake Graemsay	23 single lodger
Elizabeth Spence	Braehead Graemsay	32 single
Mary Yorston	Nicolson St Kirkwall	40 single
Margaret Dick	High St Kirkwall	50 single
Jean Leask	High St Kirkwall	40 widow ?
Isabella Garrioch	High St Kirkwall	61 widow stocking knitter
Margaret Leask	High St Kirkwall	36 single house servant lodger
Margaret Brough	High St Kirkwall	32 single
Jean Brough	High St Kirkwall	27 single
Sarah Linklater	High St Kirkwall	65 widow pauper former strawplaiter
Jessy Linklater	High St Kirkwall	30 single

Name	Address	Details
Catharine Roberston	High St Kirkwall	66 widow former strawplaiter
Catharine Roberston	High St Kirkwall	44 single
Barbara Robertson	High St Kirkwall	30 single
Elizabeth Goar	High St Kirkwall	18 single b. Stronsay
Magdaline Bews	High St Kirkwall	73 widow pauper b. Egilsay
Isabella Groundwater	High St Kirkwall	25 married b. Flotta
Helen Foubister	High St Kirkwall	30 married b. Holm, visitor
Christian Baikie	High St Kirkwall	26 single indoor servant b. Stromness
Elizabeth Drever	Union St Kirkwall	28 single
Ellen Drever	Union St Kirkwall	23 single
Elizabeth Kelday	Union St Kirkwall	25 single
Catharine Sinclair	Back St Kirkwall	46 single b. Halkirk Caithness
Elizabeth Sinclair	Back St Kirkwall	32 single b. Thurso Caithness
Mary Shearer	Palace Rd Kirkwall	48 single day labourer b. Stronsay
Janet Smith	Palace Rd Kirkwall	40 single day labourer, lodger b. St Andrews
Betsy Slater	Palace St Kirkwall	45 widow leghorn sewer b. Sanday
Margaret Slater	Palace St Kirkwall	16 single leghorn sewer b. Aberdeen
Mary Linklater	School Pl Kirkwall	36 single
Jean Ballantyne	Wellington St Kirkwall	64 widow b. Eday
Mary Mowat	Wellington St Kirkwall	16 single
Isabella Flett	Wellington St Kirkwall	18 single
Helen Robertson	Wellington St Kirkwall	78 single pauper blind b. Orphir
Janet Firth	Wellington St Kirkwall	50 single b. St Andrews
Mary Dick	Wellington St Kirkwall	54 single
Helen McKenzie	Wellington St Kirkwall	47 widow
Betsy Work	Wellington St Kirkwall	28 single b. Shapinsay
Margaret Downy	Wellington St Kirkwall	27 single b. Rousay, visitor
Mary Simpson	Main St Kirkwall	18 single bonnet maker
Mary Flett	Main St Kirkwall	37 single
Mary Hepburn	Main St Kirkwall	35 single b. Shapinsay
Elizabeth Voy	Main St Kirkwall	55 single pauper
Barbara Voy	Main St Kirkwall	53 single pauper
Betsy Muir	Main St Kirkwall	39 single b. Sanday
Christian Tait	Main St Kirkwall	53 single b Stenness
Margaret Craigie	Main St Kirkwall	51 married nee Bews
Ann Craigie	Main St Kirkwall	15 single
Margaret Chalmers	Union St Kirkwall	73 single pauper b. Canisbay Caithness
Elizabeth Guthrie	Union St Kirkwall	68 widow pauper b. Canisbay Caithness
Mary Guthrie	Union St Kirkwall	38 single

Jane Ferrier	Victoria St Kirkwall	29 single
Jane Seater	Victoria St Kirkwall	60 single pauper b. Sanday
Jane Ross	Victoria St Kirkwall	71 widow pauper b. Deerness
Catharine Flett	Victoria St Kirkwall	55 single pauper
Janet Flett	Victoria St Kirkwall	52 single pauper
Mary Laughton	Victoria St Kirkwall	28 single
Mary Merriman	Victoria St Kirkwall	34 single b. Evie bonnet maker
Jean Gorie	Victoria St Kirkwall	50 single pauper
James Marwick	Victoria St Kirkwall	86 widower ret. Strawplait manufacturer b.Rousay
David Marwick	Victoria St Kirkwall	46 single strawplait manufacturer Burgh Treasurer
Margaret Holland	Victoria St Kirkwall	59 single b. Firth
Mary Sinclair	Victoria St Kirkwall	40 married b. St Andrews
Barbra Spence	Victoria St Kirkwall	16 single b St Andrews
Jane Sinclair	Victoria St Kirkwall	7 single b St Andrews
Barbra Hepburn	Victoria St Kirkwall	27 single dress & bonnet maker b Sanday
Barbra Gorie	Victoria St Kirkwall	57 widow bonnet maker
Mary Burgess	Victoria St Kirkwall	20 single dress & bonnet maker
Margaret Moss	Victoria St Kirkwall	62 single pauper b. Rousay
Mary Work	Victoria St Kirkwall	69 widow pauper b. Westray
Betsy Sinclair	Victoria St Kirkwall	58 widow b. Westray
Marion Gaudie	Victoria St Kirkwall	74 single pauper straw sliverer
Isabella Leask	Victoria St Kirkwall	26 single straw bonnet maker
Elizabeth Garrick	Victoria St Kirkwall	26 single b. Sanday
Jane Fotheringhame	Victoria St Kirkwall	50 single
Margaret Fotheringhame	Victoria St Kirkwall	48 single
Janet Peace	Strand Kirkwall	73 widow pauper b. Sanday
Jane Peace	Strand Kirkwall	45 single
Ann Irvine	Albert St Kirkwall	24 single straw bonnet maker
Margaret Begg	Albert St Kirkwall	50 single pauper
Jane Swanson	Albert St Kirkwall	65 widow
Barbara Rendall	Albert St Kirkwall	45 single b. Stronsay
Margaret Muir	Albert St Kirkwall	23 single straw bonnet maker
Jane Shearer	Albert Lane Kirkwall	24 married straw bonnet maker b. Rousay
Ann Shaw	Albert St Kirkwall	23 single straw bonnet maker
James McBeath	Albert St Kirkwall	22 single straw plait merchant
Mary White	Albert St Kirkwall	23 single straw bonnet maker
Letitia White	Albert St Kirkwall	17 single apprentice straw bonnet maker
Jane Rendall	Albert St Kirkwall	37 single
Ann Muir	Albert St Kirkwall	15 single bonnet maker
Janet Reid	Albert St Kirkwall	38 single pauper formerly strawplaiter b. Egilsay

154

Jane Hourston	Bridge Wynd Kirkwall	28 single b. Rendall
Ann Hourston	Bridge Wynd Kirkwall	49 widow b. Rendall, visitor
Isabella Moar	Bridge Wynd Kirkwall	53 single
Isabella Bain	Bridge Wynd Kirkwall	27 single
Margaret Meal	Bridge St Kirkwall	32 single b. Sanday
Barbara Alexander	Bridge St Kirkwall	62 widow
Lydia Scarth	Bridge St Kirkwall	49 single b. Rendall
Ann Halcrow	Bridge St Kirkwall	32 single bonnet maker
Jane Linklater	Bridge St Kirkwall	46 widow b. Shapinsay
Mary Heddle	Bridge St Kirkwall	25 single bonnet maker
Barbara Petrie	Bridge St Kirkwall	30 single straw bonnet maker
Jean Walls	Harbour St Kirkwall	60 single pauper b. Sanday
Margaret Hercus	Harbour St Kirkwall	55 widow b. Sanday
Mary Corrigall	Shore St Kirkwall	34 single b Evie housekeeper
Capt Corrigall		
Jean Heddle	Shore St Kirkwall	18 single visitor
Barbara Muir	Shore St Kirkwall	51 single pauper
Hellen Muir	Shore St Kirkwall	56 single pauper
Margaret Goar	Shore St Kirkwall	34 single
Rebecca Wilson	Shore St Kirkwall	20 single
Margaret Croy	Long Wynd Kirkwall	46 single pauper b. Stronsay
Annie Walls	Long Wynd Kirkwall	21 single lodger
Mary Ann Peace	Long Wynd Kirkwall	26 single
Elizabeth Hercus	Long Wynd Kirkwall	46 single pauper b. Eday
Janet Hercus	Long Wynd Kirkwall	30 single
Mary Sclater	Long Wynd Kirkwall	45 single pauper
Amelia Greig	Long Wynd Kirkwall	58 widow b. Firth
Mary Greig	Long Wynd Kirkwall	18 single b. Firth
Margaret Groundwater	Long Wynd Kirkwall	28 single b. St Andrews
Mary Guthrie	Long Wynd Kirkwall	43 single pauper
Ann Guthrie	Long Wynd Kirkwall	36 single
Barbara Sclater	Long Wynd Kirkwall	40 widow b. Sanday
Elizabeth Bews	Long Wynd Kirkwall	47 single pauper b. Shapinsay
Jane Croy	Long Wynd Kirkwall	37 widow pauper b. Sanday
Elizabeth Turfus	Long Wynd Kirkwall	27 single
Isabella Hutchison	Long Wynd Kirkwall	53 single b. Eday
Janet Miller	Queen St Kirkwall	75 widow b. Sanday pauper former strawplaiter
Janet Scott	Queen St Kirkwall	45 widow b. Sanday
Margaret Muir	Queen St Kirkwall	46 widow b. Stronsay pauper
Margaret Muir	Queen St Kirkwall	15 single
Rebecca Sinclair	Queen St Kirkwall	40 single b. Stronsay
David Ramsay	Queen St Kirkwall	70 married b. Barry Forfarshire Agent for strawplait manufacture
Eliza Ramsay	Queen St Kirkwall	26 single agent assistant
Margaret Ramsay	Queen St Kirkwall	19 single agent assistant

Robina Linnay	Queen St Kirkwall	59 single lodger
Sibella Smith	East Rd St Catherines Cott Kirkwall	29 widow b. Shapinsay
Barbara Copland	Catherine Place Kirkwall	56 single
Elizabeth Cooper	Catherine Place Kirkwall	40 single pauper b. Stronsay
Margaret Peace	Catherine Place Kirkwall	40 married b. Sanday
Mary Peace	Catherine Place Kirkwall	18 single
Jean Moodie	Catherine Place Kirkwall	53 widow b. Sanday
Isabella Scott	Catherine Place Kirkwall	67 single pauper b. Eday
Mary Walls	Catherine Place Kirkwall	37 widow pauper b. Eday
Jane Dennison	Catherine Place Kirkwall	28 single
Margaret Heddle	Young St Kirkwall	23 single
Janet Heddle	Young St Kirkwall	21 single
Barbara Heddle	Young St Kirkwall	16 single
Jane Croy	Young St Kirkwall	20 single b. Stronsay
Margaret Tait	Quarrybank Kirkwall	43 single
Barbara Tait	Quarrybank Kirkwall	35 single
Ann Bews	Nook Kirkwall	16 single
Margaret Bremner	Caldale Farm Kirkwall	16 single
Catharine Harvey	Inverock Sandwick	34 single
Mary Merryman	Whetherstown Sandwick	18 single visitor
Jane Brass	Whetherstown Sandwick	15 single visitor
Mary Harvey	Little Room Sandwick	35 married
Betsy Brass	Room Sandwick	20 single
Catherine Spence	Kirkness House Sandwick	23 single
Margaret Hackland	Quoyloo Sandwick	56 single
Margaret Flett	Quoyloo Sandwick	48 single lodger
Mary Stockan	Quoyloo Sandwick	72 single b. Evie former strawplaiter
Catherine Moar	Lower Unigarth	38 single lodger
Margaret Garson	Mire Sandwick	38 single
Jannet Linklater	Appy House Sandwick	46 widow
Marjory Garson	Not Known Sandwick	60 widow
Janet Kirkness	Garson Sandwick	60 single
Sibella Brown	Hammerclett Sandwick	23 single straw bonnet maker
Mary Harvey	Swartland Sandwick	16 single
Mary Spence	Quoy Chreesty Sandwick	24 single
Catharine Johnston	Hill Brigg Sandwick	36 single
Ann Johnston	Hill Brigg Sandwick	24 single
Margaret Garson	Newhall Sandwick	35 single
Mary Garson	Newhall Sandwick	21 single
Ann Kirkness	Newhall Sandwick	61 single
Janet Twatt	Cott of Bea Sandwick	49 single
Ann Hourston	Quoy a Creugh Sandwick	28 single
Christina Flett	Quoy a Creugh Sandwick	61 single lodger
Christina Johnston	Break Sandwick	50 single b. Evie
Christian Hourston	Little Appyhouse Sandwick	61 single

Jean Brown	Little Appyhouse Sandwick	35 single
Catharine Russland	Hallbreak Sandwick	34 single
Elizabeth Smith	Hallbreak Sandwick	54 single visitor
Ann Linklater	Newhouse Sandwick	40 single
Margaret Linklater	Newhouse Sandwick	36 single
Jean Merriman	Queenalonga Sandwick	44 single servant
Catharine Hourston	East Break Sandwick	49 single
Ann Hourston	East Break Sandwick	47 single
Catharine Merriman	Plannan Sandwick	35 single b. Harray
Betsy Merriman	Sowamira Sandwick	26 single
Mary Merriman	Sowamira Sandwick	18 single
Ann Wishart	Howaback Sandwick	50 single retired straw cutter
Margaret Mowat	part of Mid Kirkness Sandwick	28 single b. Birsay
Mary Hackland	Hacklands Cott Sandwick	28 single
Catharine Twatt	Upper Twatts Cot Sandwick	44 single
Janet Brass	Merryball Sandwick	17 single
Barbra Moar	Hillbrae Cot Sandwick	39 single
Ann Moar	Hillbrae Cot Sandwick	37 single
Janet Stockan	Cham of Stockan Sandwick	58 single
Margaret Slater	Conziebrake Sandwick	36 single
Janet Brown	Cot of Quiena Sandwick	50 single
Catherine Louttit	Quoys Sandwick	49 single
Marjory Louttit	Quoys Sandwick	42 single
Betsy Stockan	Beggs House Sandwick	21 single
Anne McKay	School House Sandwick	45 single pauper b. Walls,Hoy
Marjory Marwick	Burwick Cot Sandwick	41 single
Elisabeth Work	Giron Sandwick	22 single
Margaret Towers	Newvoy Sandwick	20 single b. Stromness
Catherine Towers	Newvoy Sandwick	43 single b. Stromness
Janet Moar	Throat or Tot? Sandwick	47 single
Janet Merriman	Grind Sandwick	26 single b. Harray
Janet Dearness	Myrtlehall, Lady Sanday	50 single bonnet maker
Rachel Muir	Voldybrae, Cross Sanday	35 single
Barbara Sinclair	Windaway Cross Sanday	55 widow
Barbara Sinclair	Windaway Cross Sanday	19 single
Ann Work	Pool Cross Sanday	54 single beggar, lodger
Jean Sinclair	Pool Cross Sanday	45 widow b. Kirkwall
Helen Tulloch	Whippyland Cross Sanday	37 married
Barbara Scott	Schoolhouse Cross Sanday	40 single straw bonnet maker
Isabella Flett	Towerhill Burness Sanday	18 single bonnet & dressmaker
Elizabeth Spence	Upper Liddy St Andrews	24 single
Barbara Craigie	Heatherhouse St Andrews	41 widow knitter
Mary Garrioch	Willow-Vale St Andrews	20 single
Margaret Spence	Twyness St Andrews	27 single
Betsy Spence	Twyness St Andrews	20 single
Isabella Druman	Little Grind St Andrews	49 single lodger

Christian Linnay	Little Swartabrake St Andrews	53 single
Margaret Laughton	Heather Bloom St Andrews	45 single lodger
Charlotte Voy	Cringlefield St Andrews	39 single
Janet Dishon	Kerrabreck St Andrews	16 single
Margaret Muir	Road Side St Andrews	41 single
Margaret Linnie	Purtabreck St Andrews	56 single
Elizabeth Linnie	Purtabreck St Andrews	36 single
Christian Garrioch	Loch-end St Andrews	55 single
Jean Deldy	Loch-end St Andrews	30 single mistaken for her sister Betsy?
Catherine Shearer	Foxtown Shapinsay	46 single
Mary Stevenson	Waterhouse Shapinsay	24 single
Elizabeth Heddle	Heatherhouse Shapinsay	51 single
Margaret Heddle	Heatherhouse Shapinsay	49 single
Mary Work	Gateside Shapinsay	56 single b. Egilsay
Sibella Inkster	Little Gorn Shapinsay	57 widow b. St Andrews
Margaret Sketheway	Canada Shapinsay	66 married b. Egilsay
Mary Ross	St Peters South Ronaldsay	43 single hat maker
Margaret Swan	House St Peters South Ronaldsay	23 single
Betsty Stewart	House St Peters South Ronaldsay	26 single hatter of strawplait
Mina Harrold	South Cletts St Peters South Ronaldsay	22 single bonnet maker
Catherine Wood	Upper Kirk Lane Stromness	57 single b. Sandwick
Jean Robertson	Upper Kirk Lane Stromness	13 single b. Evie
Catherine Moar	Upper Kirk Lane Stromness	32 single
Jean Simpson	Upper Kirk Lane Stromness	17 single
Margaret Archibald	Upper Kirk Lane Stromness	34 single
Jean Oman	The Pleasance Stromness	28 single
Janet Murray	Queen St Stromness	37 single
Margaret Murray	Queen St Stromness	30 single
Christina Moar	Queen St Stromness	38 married b. Ceres, Fife
Hannah Firth	Queen St Stromness	39 single b. Harray
May Firth	Queen St Stromness	62 widow b. Harray
Anne Baikie	Queen St Stromness	36 single
Euphemia Baikie	Queen St Stromness	20 single
Jean Johnstone	Queen St Stromness	19 single b. Orphir
Catherine Tait	Queen St Stromness	27 single visitor straw manufacturer
Marion Inkster	Queen St Stromness	80 single pauper former strawplaiter
Cameron McKay (F)	Queen St Stromness	63 single pauper former strawplaiter
Margaret Archibald	Taits Row Stromness	24 married b. Ceres, Fife
Ann Dunnet	Taits Row Stromness	50 single b. Birsay
Janet Flett	Cloustons Close Stromness	23 single
Isabella Louttit	Cloustons Close Stromness	22 single

Jean Norn	Cloustons Close Stromness	22 single
Catherine Sabiston	Cloustons Close Stromness	20 single
John Flett	Main St Stromness	71 married b.Harray straw plait manufacturer
Catherine Firth	Main St Stromness	30 married straw bonnet maker
Margaret Flett	Main St Stromness	26 single
Margaret Sabiston	Leiths Close Stromness	16 single
Margaret Harvey	Leiths Close Stromness	53 single
Elizabeth Isbister	Millers Close Stromness	15 single b. Birsay
Ann Mowat	Main St Stromness	50 single
Christina Mainland	Kirk Rd Stromness	42 single b. Wyre
Janet Dishen	Kirk Rd Stromness	48 single and stocking knitter
John Rendall	Kirk Rd Stromness	50 married b. Evie straw plait manufacturer
May Oman	Kirk Rd Stromness	38 single
Janet Oman	Kirk Rd Stromness	43 single
Jane Fiddler	Main St Stromness	36 single?
Margaret Spence	Main St Stromness	28 single
Margaret Shearer	Snodys Close Stromness	50 widow
Robert Clouston	Main St Stromness	66 married straw plait manufacturer
Jemima Harper	Angus Close Stromness	24 single visitor
Jane Turner	Yorstons/Woods Close Stromness	30 single straw bonnet & dress maker
Elizabeth Linklater	Yorstons/Woods Close Stromness	26 single
Ann Wood	Main St Stromness	49 single bonnet maker
Christina Wylie	Main St Stromness	38 single bonnet maker
Helen Finlayson	Main St Stromness	28 widow millner & dressmaker
Isabella Clouston	Fotheringhame Close Stromness	42 single
Margaret Rich	Fotheringhame Close Stromness	51 single
Sarah Linklater	Fotheringhame Close Stromness	45 single b. Inverness
Sarah Sabiston	Fotheringhame Close Stromness	20 single
Helen Sabiston	Fotheringhame Close Stromness	17 single
Elizabeth Hackland	Johnstones Close Stromness	36 single b. Evie
Euphemia Ballantine	Taits Close Stromness	44 single b. Orphir
Clementina Gaudie	Taits Close Stromness	38 single straw bonnet maker
Elizabeth Marwick	Taits Close Stromness	22 married nee Gaudie bonnet maker
Jane McKay	Hellyhole Stromness	44 single b. Walls
Catherine Rendall	Hellyhole Stromness	48 single b. Rendall
Barbara Thomson	Hellyhole Stromness	38 single
Jane Monro	Hellyhole Stromness	46 widow b. South Ronaldsay
Christina Sutherland	Pump Well Rd Stromness	32 married bonnet maker
Ann Hunter	Pump Well Rd Stromness	59 single and knitter
Janet Maxwell	Grays Bigging Stromness	37 single

Elizabet McKay	Grays Bigging Stromness	36 single
Isabella Robertson	Spences Close Stromness	44 widow
Margaret Spence	Spences Close Stromness	28 single Milliner & dressmaker
Isabella Tait	Louttits Pier Stromness	37 single bonnet maker
Ann Clouston	Louttits Pier Stromness	63 widow b. Kirkwall
Margaret Hay	Main St Stromness	27 single bonnet maker
Susan Borwick	Main St Stromness	20 single
Joan Ballenden	Hatchhouse Pier Stromness	58 widow b. Orphir
James Sutherland	Main St Stromness	49 married b. Flotta straw plait manufacturer
Margaret Moar	Main St Stromness	17 single
Jean Moar	Main St Stromness	15 single
Jean Rendall	Grahams Pier Stromness	20 single bonnet maker
Jean Wishart	Millers Pier Stromness	54 married b. Orphir
Margaret Wishart	Millers Pier Stromness	37 single b. Orphir
Margaret Garson	Main St Stromness	45 married and seaman's wife
Catharine Spence	Main St Stromness	29 single
Betsy Spence	Main St Stromness	18 single
Anne Spence	Main St Stromness	15 single
Tomina R Brass	Louttits Pier Stromness	19 single
Jessie Flett	North End Stromness	27 single b. Harray
Janet Stanger	North End Stromness	30 married b. Birsay
Margaret Leith	North End Stromness	26 single
Barbara Corrigall	Midgur Stromness	22 single b. Walls
Mary Ann Corrigall	Midgur Stromness	18 single b. Walls
Isabella Corrigall	Midgur Stromness	13 single b. Walls
Marjory Harcus	Ness Rd Stromness	35 single bonnet maker
Jane Moar	Distillery Close Stromness	30 single and seamstress b. Kirkwall
Christina Sutherland	Distillery Close Stromness	17 single
Jane C Hardy	Upper Lane Stromness	40 single straw bonnet maker
Marjory Hardy	Upper Lane Stromness	36 single assistant straw bonnet maker
Jane Scott	Wards Close Stromness	35 single and pauper
Ann Esson	Main St Stromness	60 single
Margaret Smith	Main St Stromness	22 single straw bonnet maker
Margaret Hackland	Langhouse Stromness	22 single
Isabella Hackland	Langhouse Stromness	20 single
Betsy Hackland	Langhouse Stromness	14 single
Margaret Flett	Barebraes Stromness	14 single
Janet Hunter	Merrion Stromness	33 single
Magaret Hunter	Upper Africa Stromness	54 single
Ann Brass	Upper Arrain Stromness	49 single
Mary Sabiston	Upper Arrain Stromness	26 single
Margaret Linklater	Windiwalls Stromness	30 single
Isabella Irvine	Old Quenna Stromness	38 single

160

Susannah Irvine	Old Quenna Stromness	26 single
Hellen Irvine	Old Quenna Stromness	17 single
Catherine Irvine	Old Quenna Stromness	15 single
Isabella Irvine	Lee Stromness	37 single and farmworker
Sibella Irvine	Lee Stromness	29 single
Hellen Irvine	Lee Stromness	24 single
Robina Linklater	Little Merrion Stromness	20 single
Catherine Kirkness	Quay Stromness	43 single b. Sandwick
Margaret Kirkness	Quay Stromness	41 single b. Sandwick
Janet Towers	Redlandhill Stromness	33 single
Ann Towers	Redlandhill Stromness	29 single
Margaret Hunter	Garson Stromness	20 single
Margaret Towers	Thilohall Stromness	41 single
Ann Towers	Thilohall Stromness	38 single
Margaret Hunter	Greenfields Stromness	28 single
Jane Hunter	Greenfields Stromness	21 single
Margaret Paplay	Upper Garth Stromness	19 single
Ann Hourston	Upper Boat Stromness	28 single
Jannet Spence	Bridge End Stromness	30 single straw bonnet maker
Marjory Norn	Grassquoy Stromness	39 single b. Sandwick and agricultural labourer
Janet Norn	Grassquoy Stromness	36 single b. Sandwick and agricultural labourer
Marjory Corrigall	Seater Stromness	54 single and agricultural labourer
Catherine Brown	Maraquoy Stromness	25 married husband at Hudsons Bay
Hellen Couper	Braehead Stronsay	20 single
Isabella Sinclair	Butquoy Stronsay	29 single
Jannet Fea	Newbigging Stronsay	25 single
Mary Elphinstone	Bombasty Stronsay	64 single b. Eday and pauper
Barbara Elphinstone	Bombasty Stronsay	59 single b. Eday and pauper
Barbara Miller	Grind Stronsay	43 single
Margaret Sinclair	Blackpow Stronsay	30 single
Margaret Sinclair	Loughend Stronsay	21 single
Barbara Fergus	Eben Hall Stronsay	48 single
Elizabeth Lennie	Linksness Stronsay	30 single

Milton Keynes UK
Ingram Content Group UK Ltd.
UKHW021450280524
443385UK00049B/1577